The Expansion Factor

Debbie Forcier-Lynn

The
EXPANSION
FACTOR

Living, Leading, and Loving
from the Inside Out

The Expansion Factor: Living, Leading, and Loving from the Inside Out
© *2025 Debbie Forcier-Lynn*

Published by Thought Leader Academy Publishing
Thought Leader Academy Publishing
3901 N Kildare Ave
Chicago, Il 60641

Cover design by Claudine Mansour Design
Interior design by Liz Schreiter

Hardback ISBN: 978-1-968668-06-8
Paperback ISBN: 978-1-968668-05-1
Ebook ISBN: 978-1-968668-07-5

To every moment that cracked me open;
to every "no" that rerouted me to my truest "yes."
To the breakdowns that cleared the path
and the breakthroughs that reminded me who I am.
To the triggers, the teachers, and the tension.
To the fire I walked through and the breath that
brought me back.
To the version of me that kept showing up even
when she didn't know how.
And to every soul who walked beside me, saw,
challenged, or held space for me to expand.
This book is not just mine.
It's a tribute to the whole damn path!
Messy. Sacred. Necessary.
And the choice to rise anyway.

CONTENTS

· · · · · · · · · ·

FACTOR 1
Expand in Life—Who You Are 51

FACTOR 2
Expand in Leadership: How You Show Up 103

FACTOR 3
Expand in Love—Expand In Presence 173

The Integrating Factor
Expanding What You Came Here For 235

FORWARD
by Mike Muldoon,
President and CEO of City BBQ

I first met Debbie in 2015 at a leadership conference where she was facilitating a three-day leadership session. Shortly after, she became my executive coach —and it quickly became clear that her impact could reach far beyond one-on-one sessions. I engaged her on a broader basis, and over time, her role expanded throughout the business to include leadership training sessions, executive team coaching sessions, team coaching, and serving as a keynote speaker at our annual leadership conference.

As a CEO, I have brought Debbie into two different businesses. In both cases, she has worked across all levels of leadership. I trust her completely, not just with the development of our people, but with the heart of our leaders.

Debbie has made a meaningful and measurable difference in the lives of hundreds of our team members. Her ability to connect, challenge, and elevate others has positively transformed individuals, teams, and the culture of our organization as a whole. Put simply, she makes teams better.

So when she told me she was writing a book about expansion, about stepping more fully into who you are, how you lead, and how you love, I knew it would be more than a book. I knew it would be an experience; that's just the way Debbie operates.

The Expansion Factor is an invitation to stop chasing something "out there" and start recognizing the power we already hold. Debbie challenges us to realize that we don't need to start over or become someone new to be a great leader; we just need to come home to who we already are. Trust me; this has been one of the many challenges Debbie has given me over the years, and I have experienced the benefit in so many ways.

I often remind my team that the role we play at work is one of many roles we play in life (parent, child, sibling, leader, employee, and community and religious contributor, to name a few), and that it should not be considered the most important. Debbie addresses this head-on by reminding us that we are not a collection of separate roles we step in and out of throughout the day. We are a whole, single being, and that wholeness is where our strength lives. It lives in something she calls whole-self leadership, where these roles can be in complete alignment and not in opposition to each other.

This book is not about fixing or forcing change. It's about tuning in, looking inward, and expanding from the inside out. Expanding yourself, expanding in leadership and love—expanding the whole self. Debbie offers not just insight, but real encouragement. I can attest this encouragement is legit; believe me when I say she is cheering each one of us on to greatness and happiness. This book helps you pause and realize you already have what it takes. The journey forward does not start with a big leap. It starts with honest reflection, awareness, and the courage to grow right where you are today.

In today's fast-moving and complex world where distractions are constant and leadership advice is everywhere, it is easy to feel overwhelmed and disconnected from what truly matters. That's what makes *The Expansion Factor* so important right now. Debbie brings her years of leadership coaching and relationship building, and she distills her wisdom into clear, manageable insights. She doesn't just talk about change; she walks with you through it, offering practical tools, space for reflection, and a grounded path forward.

This book is a timely guide for anyone who wants to lead more fully, live more intentionally, and show up with heart in a world that desperately needs it. It is a call to move forward with clarity, presence, and purpose.

Debbie has told me many times over the years, "Muldoon, ask for what you want!" I now realize after reading *The Expansion Factor* that this book is exactly what I have wanted (and needed). Thanks, Deb!

WHY ANOTHER LEADERSHIP BOOK?

I asked myself that a hundred times before writing this: Does the world really need another leadership book? No, not really. But then I realized, *this isn't a leadership book.*

It's a life book.

A love book.

A show-up-as-your-whole-damn-self book.

It's about leading yourself and your life from the only place expansion is possible:

the inside out.

This is about living, leading, and loving through what I call **"whole-self leadership,"** where your beliefs, emotions, energy, and soul operate in alignment, not opposition. No more compartmentalizing who you are. No more amputating your identity at the office door.

Who you are is how you lead.

Who you are is how you love.

Who you are is what you expand.

You are always leading something.

You are always expanding something.

The question is:

What are you expanding?

FROM ME TO YOU

No Filters. No Excuses. Just Growth.

I don't know about you, but I've bought more books than I've ever finished. And for a while, I carried a bit of embarrassment about that, like maybe I wasn't "serious enough" or "disciplined enough." But one day, standing in front of a mountain of books, sticky notes, and highlighters, I had a revelation: **I'm a grazer.**

I graze through books the same way some folks graze through meals. I pick a page, take a bite, chew on it, and move on. And you know what? That's not a flaw. That's my genius.

I don't need to read from beginning to end to get what I came for. Sometimes the most important truth hits me on page ninety-three in a random paragraph I just happened to open to.

That freedom? Game-changing.

That moment of resonance? Priceless.

This book was written for the grazers. The skimmers. The seekers who don't always read in order but always read with intention. So, no matter where you are, robe on, coffee in hand, hiding in your car from your kids, or on a plane to a big-ass meeting, this book is designed for you to pick up, flip to a chapter, and walk away shifted.

Every chapter can stand alone.

Every chapter is a conversation.

Every chapter will hand you a mirror, and if you're ready, a megaphone.

You don't need to finish this book to feel it.

You just need to feel the right part of it at the right time.

We're always moving, flowing, growing . . . or we're dying.

Harsh? Maybe.

True? Absolutely.

If you're not expanding, what are you doing?

I choose growth. And for me, that looks like grazing.

That's how I want you to approach this book, too.

And don't just stop at reading. At the end of each chapter, you'll find a **thought shifter,** a journal prompt, a reflection, or an exercise. These are not add-ons. They're invitations. They're where expansion turns from a nice idea into real momentum. Because grazing without chewing? Doesn't nourish. Reading without doing? Doesn't change. This book is here to help you change.

From the inside out.

BREATHE IT IN, HOLD, AND NOW EXHALE (YOU BADASS) . . .

You didn't land here by accident. You're ready. Ready for something deeper. Ready to meet the part of yourself that's been quietly waiting. And that part? It holds your **expansion factor.** Whether you realize it or not, you're always expanding something: your beliefs, your emotions, your patterns, your life, your leadership, your love. **The Expansion Factor is the invisible driver behind what you create.** When you expand with intention, everything changes.

Stop Chasing Balance. Start Owning Alignment.

If I hear "work-life balance" one more time, I might flip a damn table.

Let's be real: **Work-life balance is a myth.**

It implies you're walking a tightrope between two lives, the professional you and the personal you. But you're not two people. You're one.

And when you try to juggle all your identities like flaming swords, something's going to drop, or worse, you're going to burn out. Balance isn't about equal weight. It's about energetic alignment.

The book you're holding will show you how to stop separating your life and start integrating it. It's your guide to showing up in every space, life, leadership, and love as the same whole, powerful, unapologetic you.

You're not holding a manual, a how-to, nor motivational fluff you toss on your shelf next to a journal you forgot existed. This book is a call-out, a call-in, and a call-forward. A mirror for your patterns. A nudge for your blind spots. And a damn microphone for your power. You'll laugh. You might cry. You'll definitely roll your eyes at least once and say, "Oof. That one was for me." You'll get science-backed truths, messy stories, real-life client stories, and tough love that doesn't pull punches.

Reading is the easy part.

Real change? That takes courage and real guts.

Expanding what you truly desire? That takes awareness, brave choices and consistent practice.

HOW TO USE THIS BOOK

Read it front to back. Flip to whatever chapter calls to you. Highlight the hell out of it. Sticky notes? Totally fine. Toss it in your bag, your bathroom, your bedside drawer. Share it with your team. Your friends. Your therapist. This book is not precious. It's practical. It's portable. It's meant to live with you, not collect dust. Use it the way you expand: Intuitively. Boldly. Authentically.

ONE LAST THING BEFORE YOU DIVE IN...

You're already expanding something. Maybe it's resentment, maybe it's courage, maybe it's fear, or maybe it's faith. Whatever it is, make it intentional. Sometimes expansion doesn't look like a big leap; sometimes it's as simple as moving the chair. This book will hand you awareness. You'll bring the courage. Together, we'll create momentum. Because you're not just here to read. **You're here to expand.** Grab a pen. Get curious. Buckle the hell up because it's time to expand in life, leadership, and love and to activate the expansion factor that's been inside you all along.

When you're ready...

Let's move the damn chair. Yeah, we'll get there, and trust me, by the time you reach the end of this book, those four words will shift everything.

THE EXPANSION FACTOR
HOW YOU GROW CHANGES EVERYTHING

Y ou are already expanding. Right now. Without even trying. Every thought you think, every belief you reinforce, every choice you make, you're feeding something. You're growing something. You're becoming something.

Expansion isn't optional.

It's not something you decide to do once you've read enough books, earned enough degrees, or survived enough storms. It's happening with or without your permission. The real power? When you realize you can choose *what* you expand. That's where the **expansion factor** comes in. The expansion factor is the invisible driver behind your life, your leadership, and your love.

It's the beliefs, emotions, energy, and soul you're expanding—consciously or unconsciously—that determine what you experience, create, and attract.

Expansion isn't about becoming someone else. It's about becoming more of who you already are beneath the survival instincts, the old programming, the fear-based habits.

You don't need to be fixed.

You don't need to be saved.

You don't need a new life.

You need a new lens. A new perspective.

In this book, you'll move through three expansion factors: three places where human beings most often get stuck and where the biggest transformations are waiting:

- **Factor 1: Expand in Life**—Who You Are
- **Factor 2: Expand in Leadership**—How You Show up
- **Factor 3: Expand in Love**—What You Receive

Each factor reveals a different piece of your expansion journey. Each factor hands you a different mirror to see yourself and a different set of tools to shift forward with power and presence. Whether you read this book front to back or jump to the section that's calling you most, one thing is certain: **You're already expanding something, so: Welcome to your expansion.**

Before you fully step into the journey of expanding in life, leadership, and love, there's one truth you need to acknowledge first: Your triggers aren't the problem; they're the portal.

The moments that make you flinch, react, or doubt yourself aren't signs that you're failing.

They're signs you're waking up. Expansion doesn't start with comfort. It starts with awareness.

It starts with honesty. It starts with learning to **see** your triggers, **feel** them, **breathe** with them, and **choose differently.**

You're not just expanding your life; you're expanding the energy that creates it.

Every thought, belief, emotion, and reaction is a seed. And expansion is the process of growing that seed into something bigger. You're either expanding fear or freedom. Protection or possibility. You're expanding from pattern into presence, from survival into alignment, from who you've been into who you're becoming.

That's exactly why we begin here. Your expansion isn't about bypassing your emotions; it's about partnering with them, listening to their messages, and turning your deepest tension into your greatest turning point. Get comfortable with the uncomfortable. Befriend your triggers. The more willing you are to meet them, the more powerfully you'll expand.

This is where your real work—and your real freedom—begins.

Now, breathe it in and here we go.

Triggered? Good. Here's Why.

Your triggers are not your enemy. They are your soul's personalized invitations to expand.

What sets you off is what sets you free. Because every trigger you feel isn't just random frustration. It's feedback. It's a flashing neon sign pointing straight at your next level of growth, wholeness, and power. Your triggers are talking. Are you listening? Expansion begins here, not in spite of your triggers, but because of them.

Triggers get a bad rap. When people hear "trigger," they immediately think:

- Anger
- Frustration
- Conflict
- Meltdown

But let's get something straight right now: A trigger is not a villain. It's not just about what pisses you off. It's an *activation*. Triggers are energy. Triggers are attention. Triggers are feedback from your soul that something in you is rubbing against something outside or inside of you. And guess what? That's not bad news. That's *great* news because your triggers are your invitations. Your portals. Your personalized wake-up calls to deeper expansion.

WHAT IS A TRIGGER?

A trigger is the collision point between energy and awareness. It's when your mind, emotions, body, and beliefs meet an experience that either *supports* your expansion or *challenges* it.

We're always expanding something. That's not the question. The real question is: **What are you expanding? Is it awareness, resilience, love, fear, control, or chaos?**

Triggers shine a light on this. If a trigger invites you to grow, take a breath, speak up, or move differently, it's an **anabolic trigger**. It pulls you into aligned expansion. If a trigger spirals you into shutdown, defense, blame, or disconnection, it's a **catabolic trigger**. It exposes misalignment and expands something you may not want: anxiety, resentment, or old stories. Both are feedback. Both are opportunities. But the power comes when you recognize what you're expanding through that trigger and whether it's serving your next level.

Here's how triggers might show up:

- A rush of joy that tells you you're on track.
- A wave of fear that begs you to stay small.
- A hit of anger that signals something needs to change.
- A pull of inspiration that dares you to rise.

The trigger isn't good or bad. It's data. It's neutral. It's the *meaning* you give it, the story you attach, that makes it feel heavy or light.

Here's what that can look like in real life: It was supposed to be a regular Tuesday. I was on my way home, groceries in the back seat, brain swirling with to-dos, when I noticed a missed call from someone I love deeply. No voicemail. Just a missed call and a short text: "Call me when you can." And instantly, it hit me like a wave.

Tight chest. Shallow breath. That old voice whispering . . . "You forgot something. You let them down. You're in trouble."

I hadn't even listened to a voicemail. There wasn't one. But my whole body reacted as if I had already failed. That's a trigger. It wasn't about the call; it was about the story the call activated: I'm not dependable, I don't show up, and I'm always disappointing someone.

That trigger didn't come out of nowhere. It was wired years ago, maybe in old family dynamics, perfectionism, or in trying to be all things to all people. Doesn't matter, really. What does matter is that in the moment, I didn't spiral. I chose to pause.

I sat in the car, hand on my chest, and said out loud, "This isn't truth. This is a story."

I breathed. I felt the fear. I traced it to its source, and I chose to cultivate something different: self-trust, clarity, and curiosity.

I called back, grounded and open. And you know what? The person just wanted to say hi. Nothing was wrong.

But *something* was revealed.

That's the power of a trigger. It's not proof you're broken. It's proof you're waking up.

YOUR TRIGGERS ARE YOUR TEACHERS

Triggers aren't here to punish you. They're here to *point you toward your next expansion.*

A trigger shows you:

- Where you're holding onto an old story
- Where your energy is misaligned
- Where your soul is craving something more honest, more whole, more real

When you run from triggers, you stall your growth. When you face them with curiosity, you accelerate your power.

THE VIBRATIONAL CONFLICT: WHY TRIGGERS FEEL SO BIG

Here's the raw truth: You can't create a new reality while obsessing over your current one.

You *know* from experience that action gets results. You've hustled. You've worked hard. You've checked the boxes. You've seen action move the needle. But action alone is not enough to create lasting expansion. When your action is fueled by fear, frustration, scarcity, or self-doubt, you're acting under a *vibrational handicap*. You're rowing upstream while dragging anchors you refuse to cut loose. Expansion is not just about what you *do*. It's about what you *believe* and how you BE. When your inner vibration, thoughts, subconscious beliefs, emotions, and energy are aligned, action becomes effortless. Inspired. Power-FULL (you, FULL of power). When they're out of alignment? Action feels heavy. Slow. Frustrating. And you get minimal results for maximum effort. Your triggers show you where that vibrational tug of war is still happening.

Like that moment in the car, my head said, "It's probably nothing." But my body? My body was bracing for bad news. That was the tug of war. One part of me expanding trust, the other still tangled in fear and ready to expand fear even further, had I not made the choice to pause.

THE PATTERN YOU'RE BREAKING

New energy is always calling you forward. But your old thoughts and beliefs (the ones you've rehearsed without even realizing it) are like stubborn roots holding you in place. Every time you try to expand, the old patterns pull at you:

- "Who do you think you are?"
- "You're not ready."
- "It's safer to stay small."
- "It's never worked before; why would it now?"

Triggers are how you *catch* those old stories trying to run the show. They are your opportunity to pause, listen, and **breathe it in.** Every trigger is asking you: What will you expand? Will you collapse back into what you've always known, or create a new way of BEing and doing?

Every trigger opens two energy doors. The question is: Which energy will you walk through?

Every trigger hands you a crossroads: A choice awaits, two doors of energy, two futures. You get to decide which one you expand.

Chaos or connection.

Sabotage or success.

Reaction or response.

Defense or curiosity.

Blame or ownership.

Shrinking or shining.

Force or flow.

Let me show you what this looks like in real life. You walk into a room, and no one looks up. Instantly, you feel invisible. That's your trigger. Now you're at a crossroads: You can walk through the door of **shrinking**—tell yourself you don't matter, fade into the background, play small. Or you can choose **standing tall**—own your energy, claim your space, speak with clarity and presence—whether they look up or not. That's the power. That's the moment. That's how you expand on purpose, not by default, but by design.

And once you've owned that kind of energy? You also get to decide if that room ever gets the privilege of your presence again.

HOW TO WORK WITH TRIGGERS INSTEAD OF AGAINST THEM

Here's the simple (but not always easy) way to turn your triggers into expansion fuel:

1. Name the Trigger

Call it out. No shame. No hiding.

"I'm feeling defensive."

"I'm feeling unseen."

"I'm feeling rejected."

"I'm feeling inspired."

"I'm feeling pulled forward."

2. Feel It Fully

Pause and **breathe it in**. Let the emotion rise without judging it or stuffing it. Your awareness is your power.

3. Get Curious

Ask yourself:

- *What belief is this trigger touching?*
- *What old story is being challenged?*
- *What new opportunity is trying to break through?*

4. Choose Expansion

Instead of spiraling into the old pattern, ask yourself:

- *How do I want to respond from my expanded self?*
- *What's the new lens I'm choosing?*
- *How can I lead with my energy, not my wound?*

YOUR TRIGGERS ARE SACRED CLUES

They're not your shame. They're not your punishment. They're not your proof that you're failing. They're your soul's GPS saying, "Right here. This is where your next level lives. **Breathe it in**. Trust the discomfort. See beyond what is . . . and reach for what is becoming."

You are always expanding something. Triggers reveal whether you're expanding fear . . . or expanding freedom.

THOUGHT SHIFTER

Befriend Your Triggers

Journal or reflect on these:

1. What's one trigger, either positive or negative, that's been showing up lately?

_____

_____

_____

_____

_____

2. What story or belief does it reveal about how I see myself or the world?

_____

_____

_____

_____

_____

3. How does that story feel in my body? (Tight, open, heavy, free?)

_____

_____

_____

_____

_____

4. What new story am I willing to believe instead?

_____

_____

_____

_____

_____

5. How will I remind myself, in real time, to **breathe it in** and choose differently next time?

_____

_____

_____

_____

_____

Inside this QR code, I've gathered my most requested and most used resources—and now they're yours for free. Step into the Expansion Portal for tools, exercises, and bonus content to help you put this book into action.

. . . .

YOUR INNER CONTRACT

THREE ALIGNMENT PRINCIPLES FOR INTENTIONAL EXPANSION

Before you dive into expanding in life, leadership, and love, there are three alignment principles I invite you to claim for yourself. These aren't rules or tasks. They're mindset anchors, soul-level shifts to guide how you lead yourself through this book and beyond. They'll challenge you. Ground you. Expand you. If you let them, they'll open the door to the kind of transformation most people only talk about.

When you're ready, begin.

ALIGNMENT PRINCIPLE ONE

YOU ARE ALWAYS EXPANDING SOMETHING

Let me show you what I mean. I once caught myself mid-scroll on social media, thinking, *Everyone else is moving faster than I am. Their stuff is better. Why even bother posting today?* I felt myself shrink. Pull back. Go quiet. And in that moment, without realizing it, I was expanding something. Not my business and certainly not my creativity. I was expanding comparison. I was expanding smallness. It hit me: Every thought, every scroll, every story I replay . . . I'm expanding something. The only question is: *what?*

You are always expanding something. That's not a cute concept. That's Truth with a capital T.

Every thought you think, every belief you reinforce, every choice you make, you're feeding something. Growing something. Becoming something.

The only real question is: **Are you expanding what serves you . . . Or what sabotages you?**

Most people think expansion is optional, deciding to grow when they read the right book, sign up for the right program, or hit the next breakthrough in their life. But here's the foundational principle:

You're already expanding.

You're always expanding.

The real power comes when you become intentional about it. Expansion doesn't wait for your permission. It doesn't require a big "aha moment." It happens with or without your awareness.

Expansion isn't a button you push. It's a state you live in. Every time you choose doubt over action? You're expanding hesitation. Every time you repeat a story that no longer serves you? You're expanding stuckness. Every time you lean into courage, truth, presence, or power? You're expanding alignment. It's always happening. The question is: **Do you even know what you're expanding right now?**

Let me take you back to a morning that cracked something open in me. It was a nothing-big, no-crisis, no-fireworks kind of day. The coffee didn't taste right; my inbox was a war zone; and my body felt like it was carrying something invisible. I walked into the kitchen, tripped over the dog's bowl, and nearly lost it. But it wasn't about the dog. Or the spilled water. Or the 42 unread emails. It was the weight I was expanding without realizing it. I was feeling resentment mixed with pressure, anxiety, and some invisible exhaustion I hadn't named yet. My chest felt it for sure. I caught my reflection in the microwave door (of all places), and I looked uptight with a clenched jaw, shoulders high, eyes dimmed. I remember thinking, *This? This isn't who I want to be. What the heck . . .* I didn't choose to feel that way that day. Not consciously. I'd just been feeding it. One choice at a time. One belief at a time. One "I've got it" when I didn't. One "I don't have time" when what I really needed was five damn minutes to consciously breathe. And that's when it hit me: *What are you expanding, Debbie?*

Pause for a second and check in. Ask yourself right now:

What energy am I expanding right now—or have I been expanding this week?

What have I been feeding in my mind, in my choices, in my reactions? Get honest. Don't answer with what you *want* it to be.

- Are you expanding clarity or chaos?
- Ownership or avoidance?
- Peace or pressure?
- Courage or control?
- Power or protection?

This isn't a judgment. This is your invitation to awareness. Because once you become aware, you can decide to shift.

AWARENESS IS YOUR POWER TO CHOOSE

Let's kill the idea that expansion always feels amazing. It doesn't. And it's not always pretty. Sometimes it's gritty. Sometimes it's uncomfortable. Sometimes it feels like everything's breaking before anything gets built. But that's part of it. Friction doesn't mean failure.

It means something's trying to move. Resistance is just the echo of your old self trying to hold on.

What if I told you you're not doing it wrong, you're just stretching.

A client once told me a story: "Debbie, I was staring at my calendar, totally frozen. I'd been putting off sending this one email for days. Not because it was hard. Not because I didn't know what to say. But because once I hit send, it meant the project was real. It meant I'd be seen. It meant people might have opinions, and suddenly, all this pressure came flooding in.

I started questioning everything: What if it flops? What if it's not good enough? What if I'm not ready? My brain knew it was just an email. But my body? My body felt like it was standing on the edge of something big. I could feel the resistance, but I also knew that resistance meant I was stretching. Not failing. Stretching. Old me would've shut the laptop and walked away. But I sat there. Took a breath. And I hit send anyway."

That moment? That's the crossroads we all hit. The stretch between who we've been . . . and who we're becoming. And it almost always appears in one of two ways: **power** or **pattern**. Let me show you the difference—not in theory, but in real-time behavior:

POWER VS. PATTERN

Power	Pattern
You respond with awareness.	You react on autopilot.
You ask what's true.	You assume and defend.
You pause to reset.	You spiral out.
You create space.	You collapse under pressure.

When you're in power, you're in choice. When you're in pattern, you're in programming. Patterns aren't bad. They're just familiar, like saying "yes" to everything because you learned early on that being needed meant being loved. They feel safe, even when they're sabotaging you. Sometimes your pattern looks like control. Sometimes it looks like people pleasing.

Sometimes it looks like "playing it safe." But "safe" isn't always aligned. Just because you can tolerate it doesn't mean it's working. Just because it's not a full-blown crisis doesn't mean it's not costing you your expansion.

MEET YOUR BRAIN'S FILTER: THE RAS

The Reticular Activating System—your RAS—It decides what gets in and what gets blocked out—based on *your* beliefs. If you believe, "I'm stuck," your RAS filters the world to prove it. If you believe, "I always screw things up," it highlights every mistake like a neon sign. But if you believe, "I'm powerful," your RAS scans for evidence to back it up.

Think of it like a search engine. Whatever you believe, your brain fetches proof to match. You don't see the whole world—you see the version your brain is filtering for.

Your brain listens to what you believe.

So if you want to expand something new, you have to feed it something new.

Write this down:

> *My brain listens to what I tell it. So I better be saying something worth expanding.*

Expansion Doesn't Mean Effortless—It Means Engaged.

Sometimes people confuse alignment with easy. But don't get it twisted: ease isn't always easy.

Alignment can feel like peace in the middle of a damn storm. Because you're alive in it. You're engaged. You're awake. Discomfort doesn't mean "stop." Sometimes it means "pay attention."

So stop trying. Start choosing. If you're still saying, "I'm trying to figure it out," what you're really doing is expanding indecision. "Trying" is a stall. It's hesitation wrapped in a bow.

Choosing, even making a micro-choice, reclaims your momentum.

Expansion Isn't Always a Thunderbolt. Sometimes It's a Challenge You Didn't See Coming.

Let me set the scene. In our office, we don't play small. We don't do fluff. And we sure as hell don't preach what we're not willing to practice. I've built a culture where feedback isn't just tolerated, it's expected. We give it. We ask for it. We challenge each other to live what we teach. If something feels off, we speak up. Period.

So when my team called me out, it wasn't in rebellion. It was in full alignment with who we are. One day, I'm on a video call with my team. We're mid-discussion, planning client work, working with our coach academy content and leadership modules, when one of them says, "Debbie, can we pause for a second?"

Now, when someone says that in my circle, I already know something real is about to drop.

They look at me, dead-on through the screen, and say: "You keep asking clients to expand, to push edges, take risks, play full out. So . . . what are you doing to expand at that level right now?"

At first, I gave the classic high-functioning, overachiever deflection: "We're good. Life is full. I'm doing plenty just by holding all this." Cue the confident nod, the slightly-too-quick smile. But they weren't buying it. And deep down, neither was I.

Because the truth was, they were right. They held the mirror up. No flinching. No backing down. And I felt it. Deep down, I knew I'd been expanding routine instead of edge, safety instead of soul. I thought I was playing full out, but really, I was playing familiar.

That challenge cracked something wide open in me. It reminded me that real expansion doesn't happen from the comfort of what you already know. It happens when you step back into the arena, not just as the coach, but as the student, too. So, I said yes. I found a new coach. I enrolled in programs that scared the hell out of me (in the best way). I got back in the arena, not just as a teacher, but as a student again. I faced the parts of me I'd been too "busy" to deal with. And that is what gave birth to this book. Not a learned theory, not a curriculum, but lived experience.

I was asking my clients to stretch, take risks, and invest in their own evolution while I was dancing in my comfort zone.

It wasn't about business. It was about embodiment. About living this work from the inside out.

Everything changed, not because I was broken, but because I was willing to be real and to stay committed to my own values: If I'm not doing it, I sure as hell can't ask anyone else to.

Expansion isn't something you teach. It's something you live. I let myself be the student again, uncomfortable, messy, vulnerable. And in that process, something powerful happened:

- I stopped expanding through hustle.
- I started expanding through belief.
- I stopped seeing myself as "someone who helps others."
- I started seeing myself as **the space-holder for expansion** because I *am* expansion.

It wasn't just my leadership that grew.
It was my marriage.
My relationship with myself.
My energy.
My emotions.
My soul.

I realized that for years, I'd been operating through filters I didn't even know were there, the "pick me" filter, the "am I enough?" filter, the "this is good enough" filter. But once I chose to expand at a soul level—not because I had to, but because I was ready to—those filters dissolved. I stopped trying to be good enough. I stopped "trying" to figure it out. I **chose** to embody it.

This is whole-self expansion.
Beliefs. Emotions. Energy. Soul.
All aligned.

All engaged.

All alive.

And that's what you're about to walk into, too, if you choose.

You don't have to change everything today. But you do have to choose something. Not because you're broken. Not because you need fixing. Because there's a bigger, truer, freer version of you already inside, waiting for you to move the damn chair and meet it. You're already expanding.

Every thought, every belief, every choice—you're feeding something.

The only question is: **What are you expanding? Is it building the life you were meant to lead?**

THOUGHT SHIFTER

Expansion Energy Check-In

Pull out your journal or pause and reflect. Gut answers only, no overthinking:

1. What energy have I been expanding lately in my thoughts, habits, and choices?

_____

_____

_____

_____

2. Is that energy aligned with the life I say I want?

_____

_____

_____

_____

3. What belief have I been unconsciously reinforcing that's keeping me stuck?

_____

_____

_____

_____

_____

4. What belief could I start practicing instead?

_____

_____

_____

_____

5. What would change first if I moved from Power instead of Pattern today?

_____

_____

_____

_____

Your Expansion Factor is already active. Now let's make it intentional.

ALIGNMENT PRINCIPLE TWO
YOU'RE NOT STUCK—YOU'RE CHOOSING

My incredible youngest child taught me this one. Not a book. Not a masterclass. Not a leadership guru. We were in the middle of one of those completely non-important moments. You know the ones, where you're standing in front of the fridge or pacing around the house, stuck between "I could" and "I should," debating decisions as if the fate of the planet depends on it. While doing this, my husband and I were knee-deep in one of our epic, back-and-forth discussions about choices, what makes them "right" or "wrong," and how regret plays into it all. We love these talks, but apparently, our then-ten-year-old was over it. Nose-deep in a book, our conversation was clearly cramping and disrupting their fantasy excursion.

With a dramatic sigh, this tiny truth-dropper cuts through all of it: "Mom, this is a choice," flashing a peace sign with their fingers and dropping them on the table. "Now just choose. Which way do you want to go? Choose and go that way. It's easy, Mom, because you'll just get to choose again." Then, back they went to their book, completely unbothered.

That moment stopped me cold. This ten-year-old's "gaming" wisdom shattered my fear of making "wrong" choices. These words, so simple and profound, flipped my brain's switch. There's no such thing as a wrong choice, just experiences that lead to the next one.

That was a jaw-dropping moment. Because I realized: *We don't get stuck because we lack clarity. We get stuck because we use "lack of clarity" as a cover for fear.* How many times have I told myself, *I need more clarity* when I really needed to trust myself? Too often, I hesitated, wasn't waiting for clarity, and was avoiding a choice. And let's be real, most of us are guilty of this. We wait for the clouds to part. For the schedule to clear. For the money to show up. For a neon sign that says "THIS WAY." But here's the thing: clarity doesn't come before the choice. Clarity comes because of the choice. Clarity is the reward for choosing.

Life is just a series of choices. Some big. Some small. Some loud. Some silent. But all of them expand something. You don't need to get it perfect. You don't need a five-step pros and cons list. You just need to choose the *next* right thing for right now. The moment you make a choice, you create momentum, which expands power.

Most people don't stay stuck because they don't have options. They stay stuck because they don't claim their agency. They don't lead their life. They wait to be chosen, approved, validated, rescued. But I am living proof that **if you don't choose, someone or something else will step in and lead for you.** And it probably won't be on your terms.

So this is your moment. Your choice. Your expansion. Your responsibility. The moment you choose, you shift the energy. And if it doesn't go the way you thought? Good news: You get to choose again.

Just like my 10-year-old said.

Simple. Direct. Powerful.

Just like expansion.

SMALL CHOICES, BIG SHIFTS

We tend to think "choice" means major life moves, quitting the job, leaving the relationship, or moving across the country. But often, it's the micro-choices that create the macro-shifts.

Choosing to respond instead of react.

Choosing silence instead of snapping.

Choosing water instead of caffeine.

Choosing five minutes of breath instead of ten minutes of doom-scrolling.

Choosing to go to bed instead of picking a fight at 11 p.m.

Tiny choices. Big ripple. Every moment is a fork in the road. And each choice nudges your life in a direction either toward alignment or away from it.

Let's just say it: **"I don't know" is a lie.** It sounds innocent. It *feels* like truth. But it's usually fear in disguise. It's your ego ducking accountability. It's your nervous system bracing for failure. It's your inner protector trying to keep you from looking stupid, messing up, or owning what you already know deep down. "I don't know" keeps you stalled when your next move is begging to be made. So stop hiding behind confusion and start listening for what's *underneath* it.

Because you *do* know. You're just scared to say it out loud. You always know. Even when you say you don't, there's a whisper. A gut feeling. A body signal. An inner pull that says, "This is the way." But most people have trained themselves not to listen to that voice. They've taught themselves to silence it in favor of logic, approval, and other people's expectations. If "I don't know" has become your go-to phrase, ask yourself: *What would I choose if I did know?*

Say it out loud. Write it down. Because that answer? It's probably already inside you. You're just scared to name it.

Fear and Freedom.

You've got two advisors at every crossroad: Fear or freedom.

Fear is loud.

It brings spreadsheets, horror stories, and "reasonable" arguments.

Freedom is quiet.

It whispers.

It invites.

It reminds you who you are.

Fear will convince you to wait.

Freedom will dare you to move.

Meet my client Lauren, who learned this the hard way. Lauren had been dreaming about starting her own wellness studio for years. She had the plan, the vision, the certifications, the client base, all of it. But every time she got close to taking the leap, fear grabbed the mic.

Fear said:

What if no one shows up?

You've got a great job, don't screw it up.

What will your dad think? You're not smart enough to make money as a business owner of a wellness studio; people are not interested in that.

And so she stayed put, polishing the plan and tuning the website that never launched. She asked for feedback, but she didn't really want it. She called it "being strategic." I called it what it was: *expanding fear*.

Then, one day, the corporate job she had clung to for "safety" laid her off. There was no warning, no backup plan. The thing she feared most happened anyway, and guess what? She survived it. Not only that, but within two months, she launched the studio. And within six, she had a waitlist.

When we talked later, she said, "Debbie, freedom was whispering the whole time. I just kept telling it to shut up while fear shouted."

Ouch, the lesson was learned the hard and long way. Fear loves data. Freedom loves decisions. And expansion? It follows whichever one you let lead.

You'll never be "not afraid." That's not the goal. The goal is to stop letting fear make your choices for you. So the next time you're in that "I don't know what to do" space, ask:

Who's driving this decision . . . fear or freedom? Then choose accordingly.

YOU'VE ALREADY CHOSEN MORE THAN YOU REALIZE

You chose to read this book. You chose to engage with this idea of expansion. You chose to be curious, brave, maybe even a little pissed off at some of these truths, and you're still here.

That means something.

That means you already know how to choose.

Now it's just about doing it with intention and purpose.

THOUGHT SHIFTER

The Choice Audit

Grab your journal, notes app, or a napkin. Doesn't matter—just reflect:

1. What's one decision I've been stalling on? What is it costing me?

_____

_____

_____

_____

2. What do I already know that I've been pretending not to?

_____

_____

_____

_____

3. What's the smallest choice I could make today that would move me toward alignment?

_____

_____

_____

_____

4. Who have I been outsourcing my decisions to?

_____

_____

_____

_____

_____

_____

5. What would I choose right now if I believed I were safe to move?

_____

_____

_____

_____

_____

_____

You don't need clarity.
You don't need confidence.
Just like that kid said, *just choose.*

ALIGNMENT PRINCIPLE THREE

ALIGNMENT STARTS WITH KNOWING WHAT MATTERS MOST

Have you ever watched someone carry an entire department on their back while the team's leader is mentally packing for retirement?

I have.

A few years ago, I was coaching a brilliant director at a company where the team dynamics had eroded entirely. The leader above him (let's call him Jim) was in glide mode, counting down the days to retirement. He was half-in, half-out. Technically, he was still present, but it was clear the only thing he was managing anymore was his golf game.

Meanwhile, my client (let's call him Marcus) was picking up every loose piece. He stayed late, triple-checked reports, calmed down frustrated employees, and covered for missed deadlines. He was carrying the department so the numbers didn't slip, and here's the most frustrating thing for him: He wasn't even getting credit for it. When I asked him why he was pushing so hard, he shrugged and said, "Because someone has to."

Sounds noble, right? But I saw a man expanding burnout in the name of being a team player. When we dug deeper, it turned out Marcus didn't even *want* to be in that role long-term. He had dreams of building something entirely different, but he'd lost the thread of what mattered to him. Why? Because he was operating from someone else's values. He had absorbed Jim's passivity, the team's chaos, and the company's unspoken rule that "numbers matter more than people." And in the process, he sacrificed his values of connection, joy, and autonomy all because he didn't want to drop the ball.

So, I asked him: "If you keep expanding this version of leadership, what does your life look like five years from now?" He paused, looked away, and said, "Honestly? It looks like exhaustion. Resentment. And a version of success that doesn't even feel like mine." That moment? It shifted everything because Marcus got clarity. He realized if you don't get clear on what matters most to *you*, you'll unconsciously expand what matters to everyone else.

If you don't know what matters to you, you'll follow what matters to everyone else. You'll say yes when you mean no. You'll pursue goals that aren't even yours. You'll build a life that looks successful but feels like a prison.

Knowing your values isn't about being virtuous. It's about being rooted. And your "why"? That's not just for entrepreneurs and TED Talks. Your "why" is your inner compass. It's the reason you show up even when it's hard. It's the reason you say no even when you're tempted.

Your values and your why? They're how you stop chasing and start choosing.

WHAT YOU VALUE CREATES WHAT YOU EXPAND

If you say you value peace but you constantly expand chaos. . .

If you say you value integrity but you keep breaking promises to yourself. . .

If you say you value connection but you constantly self-isolate. . .

Then there's a gap. And that gap creates friction. Friction is a signal. It doesn't mean you're broken. It means you're out of alignment. Your *expansion* is only sustainable when it's built on what you truly value, not what you were taught to value, not what your job rewards, and definitely not what gets the most likes on social media.

Don't Just List Values. Feel Them.

Most people treat "values" like a vision board exercise. They pick words like honesty, compassion, courage, and post them on a wall. But values aren't Pinterest quotes or wall-worthy, printable statements. They're daily filters for your choices, actions, and energy.

Here's how you know something's a true value: You feel the friction the moment you violate it. And you feel deep satisfaction when you honor it, even if no one sees it. You don't have to "try" to live a true value. It lives *in* you. You just have to get quiet enough to remember it.

Let's go a level deeper. Under every real value is a *why*, and often, under that is even a deeper *why*. Here's another thing: Sometimes our values start in fear. We think we value something, but really, it's a protective response. A survival strategy.

Let this example shine some light on this: You say you value freedom. Cool. But let's dig deeper. Is it truly freedom you value, or is it the feeling of escape from something that once hurt you? Perhaps you spent your childhood trying to fit in, felt trapped in a past relationship, or were raised in a system where rules reigned and self expression was stifled. All of that is valid. But it might not mean freedom is your core value. It might just be the reaction. That's the fear layer. The protection layer. The "I need to run from this" response is disguised as a value.

Now, here's the opportunity: Go deeper. Ask again, *If I didn't need to protect myself, what would I value then?* You might still land on freedom, because it feels like truth, expression, aliveness, and purpose. Or you might land somewhere else entirely. Maybe it's belonging, perhaps it's trust, creativity, love, stillness, or ease. That's the love layer, the one that's not reacting to your past, but creating from your soul. Your real values don't scream for safety. They speak in clarity, not panic. And when you meet them there, your expansion stops being a reaction and becomes a homecoming.

Let's do another one. You say you value honesty. Okay . . . but why? Because you used to lie to survive? Because someone betrayed your trust, and now you guard the truth like a vault? Because you were taught to stay quiet, nod along, and keep the peace? Those might feel like values, but let's get real—that's not alignment. That's survival. That's fear wearing the mask of virtue. Now go deeper and look at some love-based whys. Maybe honesty feels like alignment, clean, clear, no mental gymnastics. Maybe honesty is your way of building safe, sacred relationships that actually mean something. Maybe honesty is how you sleep at night, pillow meets peace, not performance. That's the root. That's the real. And if it's not? That's okay, too. Sometimes, when you peel back the fear, you find that the truth isn't honesty at all. It's belonging, or freedom, or *self-respect*. Honesty was just the fence you put up to keep the pain out.

Your values aren't random. They're shaped by experience, but they're defined by **truth**. When you reconnect with the love underneath the fear and find the *real* why, you remember your fire. And that's what fuels aligned expansion. You can chase growth all day long, read the books, hire the coach, and crush your goals. But if your expansion isn't built on values, you're just building faster in the wrong direction. Expansion without values is just hustle, and hustle without alignment? That's self-abandonment in disguise.

Just like Marcus, who was hitting the numbers, holding the team up, looking like a rockstar from the outside. But inside? He was disconnected from himself, burning out while carrying the weight of everyone else. He *said* he valued teamwork. *Said* he valued loyalty. But what he was really expanding was resentment, exhaustion, and performative success. His true value and well-being had quietly been sacrificed at the altar of productivity. That's the danger of unchecked expansion. It might look like success, but it feels like a slow unraveling. You weren't meant to hustle your way into someone else's definition of success. You were meant to expand into a life rooted in who you actually are. And that begins the moment you stop performing and start aligning. Not for applause but for peace, for presence, for power. Your power.

Not Sure What You Value? Start With These Questions:

- When was the last time I felt deeply in alignment? What was I doing? What value was I honoring?
- What's something that makes me feel off even when it looks "right" on paper?
- What choices do I regret? What value did I betray in making them?

- What values do I pretend to have to fit in that don't actually feel true for me?

Your values live underneath your reactions, decisions, triggers, and joy. If you slow down and pay attention, you'll find them.

VALUES IN ACTION = ALIGNED EXPANSION

I had a client once who was sharp, driven, and everyone's go-to for getting things done. She had a goal to climb the corporate ladder. On paper? She was killing it. Promotions, praise, power suits. But behind the scenes, she was burnt out, disconnected, and flatlined in joy. In one of our sessions, I asked, "Why this ladder?" She blinked, paused, and then said, "I don't know. I guess because everyone expected me to." It turned out it wasn't her ladder; it was her father's dream, her mentor's roadmap, and her old, approval-chasing self doing what looked impressive but felt empty.

So she did the boldest thing I've seen someone do with a six-figure salary and a LinkedIn full of clout. She quit. Not in a dramatic storm-out way, but in a grounded, soul-led, "I'm choosing me now" kind of way. And what did she do? She traveled abroad for six months. She had family in Europe and used that time to reconnect with her childhood, her roots, and her passion. When she came home, she opened a bakery, a cozy, wildly creative space where she wakes up at 5 a.m., not to grind pavement, but to grind fresh coffee and bake cinnamon rolls that sell out before noon. She plays her favorite music, greets her regulars by name, and finally feels like her life matches her values: creativity, connection, joy. Her expansion didn't shrink her success. It redefined it.

Oh, and her dad? He's her first customer most mornings now. Because that's what aligned expansion does. It stops being about proving something. It starts being about living something.

Knowing your values isn't enough. You must *live* them. That means making choices that feel right for *you*, even if they don't make sense to anyone else. That means saying no when it would be easier to people please. It means letting go of a goal that no longer lights you up, even if it once did. When your values drive your choices, your expansion becomes sustainable. It stops being a performance. It becomes embodied.

THOUGHT SHIFTER

The Alignment Map

Take ten minutes. Reflect honestly. Write it down.

1. What are the top three values I actually live by (not just what I wish I lived by)?

_____

_____

_____

_____

_____

2. What's a value I've been ignoring or minimizing? How is that affecting me?

_____

_____

_____

_____

_____

_____

3. Where do I feel the biggest gap between what I value and what I'm currently doing?

_____

_____

_____

_____

_____

_____

_____

_____

4. What "shoulds" am I mistaking for values that actually aren't mine?

_____

_____

_____

_____

_____

_____

_____

_____

_____

5. What would a day look like if I filtered all my decisions through my values?

_____

_____

_____

_____

_____

_____

_____

_____

_____

_____

_____

_____

_____

_____

_____

_____

_____

You don't need to get it perfect. You just need to get honest. Know your values. Know your why.

And start expanding on purpose.

So, what have you agreed to?

1. **You're always expanding something:** Might as well make it intentional. Feed the energy that fuels you, not the junk that drains you.

2. **You're not stuck; you're just stalling:** Own your choices, stop hiding behind "I don't know," and pick a damn direction. You can always choose again.

3. **Your values are the real GPS:** If you don't know what matters most, you'll end up living someone else's version of "success" and wondering why it feels so damn heavy.

These three agreements? They aren't rules. They're your anchor points. Your recalibration tools. Your expansion contract with yourself. Now let's get to it. Page by page. Choice by choice. Breath by breath. Let's expand in life, leadership, and love from the inside out.

FACTOR 1

· · · · · · · · · ·

EXPAND IN LIFE— WHO YOU ARE

You must begin at the beginning *and* the end, because both are the same place: You.

Before you expand your leadership, before you expand your love, you have to expand *yourself*.

Not the version you perform. Not the one you protect. The real you, rooted, honest, and fully plugged in. You are the root system. You are the energy in the room. You are the common denominator in every relationship, every decision, every dream. Nothing changes if you don't.

So this is where we start. Not out there. *In here.* This isn't about fixing your life. It's about claiming it. All of it. The beautiful parts. The messy parts. The parts that are still under construction.

Life expansion isn't about adding more to your plate. It's about becoming more awake to the life you're already living and deciding what parts of it deserve your energy now.

In this factor, you'll explore:

- How your beliefs, emotions, and patterns are expanding something, right now
- How to shift from surviving your life to leading it
- How to recognize when you're operating from power versus when you're trapped in a pattern
- How to expand your life from the inside out, not by efforting harder, but by aligning more deeply

Ready to meet the next version of you? Guess what, you don't have to burn it all down to build something beautiful. You just have to get conscious about what you're expanding.

Before we dive into this next phase, let's pause for a hot sec.

If you read the three alignment principles before this chapter (and I hope you did), then you already know: This book doesn't play by traditional rules. We didn't start with Chapter 1 because you didn't need another surface-level pep talk. You needed truth. You needed a mirror. You needed to set the foundation, and those three alignment principles? That was your soul prep.

You've already been reminded that:

- You are always expanding something.
- Life is a series of choices.
- Alignment starts with knowing what matters most.

Without those anchors, we'd be building your expansion on sand. And I'm not here for flimsy foundations. So now . . . we begin. But not the way you've been taught to. We're not starting from clarity. We're not waiting for motivation. We're not pretending things need to be perfect first. We begin where you are, even if you're tired, even if you're tangled, even if you're still side-eying the word "expansion."

Let me tell you how this chapter was born: I was on a video call with a client who wanted to "live differently." She said, "I'm ready. I just don't know where to begin." My answer? "Begin where you are, even if it's messy." She laughed, then cried, because that was the beginning. There was no plan, no clarity, just a moment, and in that moment, she gave herself permission to move.

This section is not a roadmap or a reset, but a reclaimed moment of truth. This is the moment where you begin, in whatever state you're in, with what's real, what's possible, and what's next.

CHAPTER 1

BEGIN WHERE YOU ARE— EVEN IF IT'S MESSY

It was a Friday. Not just any Friday, it was *Debbie's Choice* day. No calls. No sessions. Just me, my coffee, and this book—yep, the one you're holding—ready to pour itself out of me like divine inspiration in yoga pants.

I had it all planned out. I even got up before the sun (like a damn author-warrior) and tiptoed to the kitchen like a ninja so I wouldn't wake the dogs or my husband. Because if they're up, my day is no longer mine—it's fetch, feed, find-the-leash, and talk-about-the-lawn time.

First cup of coffee in hand, I sat in my favorite chair—the cozy one that makes me feel like I'm about to write something profound—and just breathed it in. *This is it. Today is THE DAY.*

Except . . . second cup time rolled around, and the sabotage began.

The dishwasher was full. *I'll just unload it real quick.*

Sugar bowl was empty. *Might as well refill it.*

Kitchen table had crumbs. *Wipe that down—I mean, what kind of monster leaves a sticky spot?*

Cue dogs. All three. Staring at me like I owed them an apology and a bacon strip. So we did our morning snuggle-fest, which turned into a "let me just sweep the porch while I'm out here," which turned into folding laundry, watering a plant I don't even like, and making sure my husband got up, chatted, got his list going, and felt fully supported—like the domestic goddess I apparently decided to cosplay as that morning.

Five a.m. became 10 a.m., which became noon. Noon became *holy hell, it's 2 p.m., I haven't written a word, I've got a 5 o'clock dinner date, and I'm still in pajama pants with one sock on.* I sat down, finally, laptop open, iced tea in hand, and thought, *How did I expand everything but my intention?* And that, my friend, is where this chapter begins. Because here's what I know to be real. This wasn't laziness. It wasn't confusion. It was fear dressed up as productivity. It was avoidance in a power suit. We think we're waiting for clarity, but what we're really doing is delaying the moment we meet ourselves on the page, in the mirror, or in the damn chair. That's why I say, stop trying to find the perfect place to start. We all do this in some form or fashion. So . . . Start where you are, even if the sugar bowl's still empty. Let it stay empty.

The belief that you have to get everything figured out first before you create the expansion you want is just a fancy way of saying, "I'm scared to move." You don't need a full-blown plan. You don't need to quit your job, change your name, or book a flight to Bali. You just need to breathe in and exhale, right where you are with what you've got. In the middle of whatever it is you're in and whatever you are doing.

If you're waiting for clarity to arrive, you might be scrambling for a while. Clarity is often the result of movement, not the prerequisite. I didn't need confidence that morning; I needed permission. My permission. If you are feeling a twinge of anxiety about what to do, what this will require of you, and whether you will be able to "do" it? What you might really be asking is: "When will I feel safe, excited, or comfortable enough to move and make this happen?" Welp, here's another one of those truth bombs for you to write on a sticky and put on the fridge or on your desk: *That feeling doesn't show up until after you choose to begin.*

When my "book day" turned into everything-but-the-book day? It wasn't just about procrastinating. It was about energy. I was standing on the edge of a vision I could *feel* but couldn't quite *see* yet, a dream that had been whispering to me, *"Hey, I'm in here . . . come find me."* But instead of walking toward it, I started loading the dishwasher.

Sound familiar? My head didn't know there was procrastination from fear of doing or fear of failing, but my beliefs and emotions did, resulting in my actions playing it all out.

Whether it's your book, your business, your body, your relationship, or just that wild, sacred knowing that you're meant for more, expansion doesn't show up fully formed. It starts like a flicker—a gut pull, a half-formed idea that you know matters, but that you can't quite articulate yet.

Instead of letting ourselves sit in the discomfort of *almost*, we distract ourselves with dishes, with "urgent" emails, with scrolling, and with everyone else's needs. We subconsciously wait or tell ourselves, "I just need to feel it first . . ." but what we're really doing is expanding hesitation, not the dream. So here is a shift for you: You're not just expanding a to-do list; you're expanding a frequency, a future, and a vision that's waiting on your energy to match its momentum. So yeah, the sugar bowl might still be empty. But the dream? She's sitting on the porch with her coffee, waiting on you.

Real life doesn't pause so that you can start your self-growth journey. You don't get to hit a magical reset button where the kids are calm, the job slows down, the money flows, and all your doubts disappear. Stop waiting for the clean slate. Beginnings aren't about *tidiness*. They're about truth. You don't need a clear runway. You need a grounded reason.

That reminds me of something Claire, a client who came to me with fire in her eyes but bricks on her chest, said: "Debbie, I want to do this work. I want to expand toward the life I want, not being robbed by what everyone else wants. But I'm so maxed out, so compartmentalized. I feel like if I move one inch the wrong way, I'll blow my whole life up. I can't afford to fall apart right now."

Whew. I felt that. So we didn't start with massive shifts. We started with one quiet, radical move: permission. Permission to tell the truth. Permission to not have it all figured out. Permission to feel without fixing. And, little by little, Claire stopped trying to hold it all together with duct tape and denial. She started *leading* her life again, not reacting to it. She restructured her mornings. Had one real, messy conversation with her partner. Gave herself thirty minutes of space that was hers, no matter what. And you know what happened? She didn't fall apart. She came alive. Because she didn't need to blow her life up, she needed to breathe in it.

Expansion didn't demand perfection. It just asked her to stop abandoning herself. And once she did, everything began to shift. This difference? It was now, on her terms, with her power.

Want to know the best place to start? Start with what's true. Start with what's right in front of you. Start with the smallest aligned move you're willing to make, *and repeat it.*

That might look like:

- Drinking a full glass of water before coffee.
- Leaving your phone in the other room for 20 minutes.
- Taking one conscious breath before responding to that text.
- Saying "no" without justifying it.
- Saying "yes" to something you've been avoiding.

Expansion doesn't need to be dramatic to be powerful. It just needs to be intentional and have purpose. However, be ready, for oftentimes, the moment you even *think* about beginning, resistance will show up. But your resistance doesn't have to be a roadblock; it can be your signpost. It could sound like:

- "Now's not the right time."
- "I'm too tired."
- "This isn't a big enough step."
- "What's the point?"

That's not a red flag. That's recognition. Your system is used to the current version of you.

So when you try to begin something different, even if it's better, your subconscious says, "Whoa whoa whoa, we don't do that here." Don't fight the resistance. Don't wait for it to disappear. Just recognize it, thank it for trying to protect you, and then . . . move anyway with a reframed thought or belief.

It could sound like:

- "This timing feels uncomfortable; it might be exactly when I need to stretch."
- "My energy matters. What's one small, aligned step I *can* take with the energy I have?"
- "Every aligned step counts, even the small ones create momentum."
- "If this stirs something in me, that *is* the point; it's calling me forward."

There's no single path. No magic sequence. No secret playbook for expansion. Stop looking for the "right step" and take any step that is true for you. Maybe that is you simply asking for help, saying no to something that drains you, rewriting a belief that's been running your life, or getting quiet long enough to hear what's actually your inner voice.

Every powerful, aligned, soul-on-fire person you admire started somewhere that felt small, weird, or messy. Nobody begins with momentum. They begin with a moment. One breath. One boundary. One brave-ass move.

You begin the moment you decide to, and that's when you're intentionally expanding. The results may not be visible until later. This isn't about what you do. It's about what you decide.

It's the moment you say:

- "I'm not available for this version of my life anymore."
- "I'm not shrinking for safety."

- "I'm not playing pretend just to fit in."
- "I'm not outsourcing my worth to anyone else."

Your expansion sparks the moment you reclaim your power, not because everything is figured out but because you're *done waiting*. You're not late. You're not behind. You're not broken. You're just *right on time* to begin.

THOUGHT SHIFTER

Your Starting Point

Write it out. Speak it aloud. Make it real:

1. What truth have I been ignoring because it might require a change?

2. What's the smallest aligned action I'm willing to take today and repeat tomorrow?

3. What excuses am I still letting drive the car?

_____

_____

_____

_____

_____

_____

4. What would beginning look like if I didn't need it to be impressive, just real?

_____

_____

_____

_____

_____

_____

5. What fear is trying to stop me—and what freedom is calling me forward?

_____

_____

_____

_____

_____

You don't need a plan. You need a beginning. Let this be it.

. . . .

CHAPTER 2

YOUR ENERGY SPEAKS— ARE YOU LISTENING?

Did you know you are an energetic being? And whether you know it or not, you're always communicating something, long before you open your mouth. For instance, ever walked into a room and *felt* someone's stress before they even said hello? Or known your partner was pissed from the way they closed the cabinet door? Yeah, that. Energy talks, and it talks loudly if we listen closely. Your presence speaks. Your posture speaks. Your tone, your breath, your stillness, your urgency—they all speak loud and clear, and they send messages. The most powerful leaders, lovers, parents, partners, and humans? They own their energy before they try to direct anyone else's.

We've all felt it: Someone walks into a room and the entire vibe shifts. You feel tension before it's named. You feel warmth before a single word is spoken. That's not magic. It's science, actually, and . . . it's *energy*. Your energy is your unspoken signature. It introduces you before your words ever will. It's your silent invitation or your unconscious warning. And if you're not owning it, then it's owning *you*.

ENERGY IS CONTAGIOUS, AND YOU'RE EITHER SPREADING CLARITY OR CHAOS

You don't have to say a word to change a room. But if you're unaware of your energy, you might be leaving a trail of chaos without even realizing it. Have you ever walked into a meeting and suddenly felt heavy, anxious, or weirdly defensive? You were just handed someone else's energy, like a virus. Now flip it: Have you ever been around someone so grounded, so clear, that you naturally slowed your breathing? That's an energetic influence also, and we all have it.

You are either influencing or being influenced. And the difference is awareness.

RESPONSIBILITY ≠ PERFECTION

This isn't about being "high-vibe" 24/7. You're human; you'll get annoyed, have off days, and show up messy. Owning your energy doesn't mean controlling it or faking it. And don't even get me started on that phrase, "Fake it till you make it." Where the heck did that even come from? And why did we let it go viral? Your energy will not let you fake anything except *yourself.*

Let me tell you about Melissa. She was a senior leader who looked the part, always polished and "on." Could sell a strategy like nobody's business. But her team? They weren't buying it.

I got called in because there was friction, high turnover, low engagement, people smiling in meetings and checking out the second the Zoom ended.

In our first session, Melissa came in with all the right words:

"I just want to make sure my team feels supported."

"I've been working on being more empathetic."

"I really value open communication."

Sounds good, right? Except that the energy was tight. She sat rigid. Smiled with her mouth, but not her eyes. She gave answers as if she were checking boxes, not actually connecting.

So I asked her, "Melissa, how *are* you, really?" The truth cracked through. She exhaled like she'd been holding her breath for months and said, "Honestly? I'm exhausted. I feel like if I take my foot off the gas for even a second, everything will fall apart. But I can't let them see that. I'm the leader. I have to hold it together."

There it was. She wasn't leading. She was performing. And her team could feel it because energy doesn't lie. It leaks. They weren't resisting her leadership; they were mirroring her fear.

And when we finally let her *drop the mask* and reconnect with herself, her team started to rise.

Not because she got more polished, but because she got real. That's the power of energy ownership. It's not about faking calm. It's about becoming safe enough in your own presence that people can breathe around you. It's not about perfection. It's about presence. People don't follow what you say; they follow who you are.

Owning your energy means being responsible for it. Being aware of what you're bringing into the space, and choosing whether that's what you actually want to bring.

Responsibility doesn't mean perfection. It means intention. I feel I have to state this because energetic awareness isn't woo, it's Leadership with a capital "L." You don't need sage or crystals to take your energy seriously (though if that's your thing, go for it). This isn't about spirituality at the moment. It's about congruence. Are your words, actions, and energy saying the same thing? If your mouth says, "I'm open to feedback," but your body is shut down and tense, people will feel the truth, not the script. If you say "I'm over it," but your vibe is still stuck in resentment, people will respond to the energy, not your words.

Owning your energy is the difference between performative leadership and embodied presence. Another way to say it: Stop "acting" and putting on a show, just *be* what you want others to *be*.

Every one of us has an energetic set point, a frequency we fall back into when we're not being intentional. For some, it's anxiety. For others, it's urgency. Some default to people-pleasing energy. Others, to defensiveness or control.

Your set point—that default emotional state you keep falling back into—wasn't born with you. It was programmed. Shaped by your early definitions of safety. Shaped by the rules you didn't even know you were following. Shaped by the unspoken agreements your nervous system made when life felt too big, too fast, or too much. And here's what I've learned by living this energy work, not just teaching it: When I mess up (and yes, I still do), I've trained myself to ask:

"What taught me that?"

"What energy was I expanding when I made that move?"

"How do I shift this to something that actually feels aligned with the me I'm becoming?"

Then I move. Sometimes quickly and sometimes slowly, but I move forward, even if it's just one breath closer to the truth.

Because here's the actual good news:

Your set point is programmable.

It can be rewired.

It can be upgraded.

It can be owned by you, rather than you being dragged around by it.

You're in charge until you forget, then you remember, and then you repeat. That's the practice.

Shifting doesn't require a full-on spiritual bulldozer moment. It starts with something deceptively simple: **noticing.** So what does that actually mean?

Here is a practice you can start with today, right now:

- **Notice your body.** Is your jaw tight? Shoulders up? Gut clenched? Chest swirling or tight? That's your energy signaling you're out of alignment before your brain even catches up.
- **Notice your vibe.** Are you storming into a room trying to control the outcome? Or are you grounded in what you came to contribute?

- **Notice your residue.** What are people left with after they interact with you? Relief? Clarity? Tension? Confusion?
- **Notice your mismatch.** Are you saying "I'm fine" but vibrating frantic? Leading a team while leaking resentment? Smiling while secretly stewing?

This isn't about judging yourself. It's about tuning into the energetic ripple you're creating and choosing if that's what you actually *want* to expand.

Then pause.

Breathe.

Recalibrate.

Ask: **"What energy do I want to lead with right now?"**

This isn't about perfection. It's about presence. Because the second you become conscious of your energy, you've already taken your power back.

This isn't about getting it right. It's about showing up awake, mindful, and present. Energy isn't about being loud; it's about being clear. Some people think owning their energy means being the biggest, boldest person in the room. But real energetic ownership isn't about volume; it's always about awareness and clarity. Each can be soft. They can be still, calm, and commanding at the same time. When you own your energy, you stop leaking it. You stop defending it. You stop performing it. You just *become it.*

YOU DON'T HAVE TO MATCH THE ROOM, YOU CAN CHANGE IT

Read that again. You don't have to match the dysfunction, the fear, the chaos, or the urgency.

You don't have to shrink yourself to soothe the egos. You don't have to mirror other people's energy to be accepted. You get to *bring* the energy you want to feel. And that becomes the invitation for the room to rise with you. That's the difference between being a thermometer and being a thermostat. One reflects the temperature. The other sets it.

Let me show you what this looks like in real life.

A few months ago, I had a client; let's call her Michelle. Michelle was walking into executive meetings like she was preparing for battle, heart armored, shoulders braced, energy zipped up tight. The moment she sat down, she matched the room: cold, analytical, detached. Why? Because *that's what they did*. It was all strategy, no soul. And she thought the only way to stay in the room was to mute her magic. Until one day, she didn't. She walked in with a different energy, *her* energy. Still sharp and smart, but this time, she didn't armor up. She grounded. She softened her tone without losing her strength. She asked a real question instead of powering through her bullet points. She paused. She breathed. She *listened*.

The wildest thing happened. The room shifted. People leaned in. The tension dropped.

One exec literally said, "This feels different. I think we've been missing this." And they had. But more than that? She had. The real her had been missing. That's what happens when you stop trying to match the room and decide to influence it. You stop blending in. You start expanding the truth.

You're not here to mimic the energy around you. You're here to *lead* it. So the next time you feel that urge to match the chaos, the urgency, the emotional shutdown?

Don't.

Take a breath.

Set your tone.

Lead from your aligned energy. Because the moment you own the energy you bring, you stop surviving rooms and start transforming them. That's how you expand your impact. Not by playing it safe. But by playing it real. Now go be the damn thermostat. The room is waiting.

THOUGHT SHIFTER

Energy Audit

Slow down and get real:

1. What is my default energy in high-stress or high-stakes situations?

_____

_____

_____

_____

2. What energy do I bring into my relationships? Is it helping or hindering connection?

_____

_____

_____

_____

3. What's the vibe I want to be known for?

_____

_____

_____

_____

4. Where am I leaking energy trying to manage other people's reactions or approval?

_____

_____

_____

_____

_____

5. If I walked into a room as my most grounded, embodied self, what would that feel like? What would shift?

_____

_____

_____

_____

_____

You don't need more confidence. You need *congruence*. Listen and own your energy, and expansion will follow.

Energy isn't just something you feel; it's something you can *track*, *shift*, and *master*. In an upcoming chapter, I'll walk you through the exact model we use with clients to do just that. But first, let's explore how your brain and your beliefs are reinforcing the patterns that keep you stuck.

. . . .

CHAPTER 3

I SEE ME—OWNING
THE MIRROR

Want to change your life? Change how you see yourself.
Not the polished, professional, "I've got it all together" version. I mean really see yourself, raw, real, and in the places that still make you flinch. Because what you see is what you get. Your beliefs shape your perception. What you focus on, you expand.

I'll never forget the moment this hit me. I was sitting in coaching school, silently judging the content. *This is too simple. I need something deeper, more intense, more powerful,* I thought. I was so busy critiquing the message that I was missing the experience until, out of nowhere, this poem poured out of me like lightning from my soul.

That was what I call my "mirror moment." I saw my own truth and my own blocks, and I saw that what I see in others . . . is what I carry within myself.

I will say that again for you: What you see in others . . . is what you carry within yourself. If it weren't there, you couldn't see it.

I SEE ME (POEM)

What do I see when I see you?
I see me, in thee, in you, I see me . . .
Do you make me smile or do you make me cringe?
It's not you, IT's me then . . .
If I did not have in me the pain I see,
Then who would I be? I'd be me . . .
When I'm angry, from where has it come,
Why does it reside?
"I don't know," I may say . . .
But knowing is where my freedom is this day . . .
Wishing others would see the way I see
This is not for me . . .
It only confirms what I see . . .
So, when I look at you, what do I see?
I see me . . .

That was a moment, no doubt, as I sat and reread what just flowed out of me onto the paper. And the truth? The learning didn't stop there. It still shows up to this day. Self-projection? It's just a mirror, and we are looking in with our own masks on. We try to label what we see in others as their issue, their drama, their dysfunction, their energy. But here's the real talk: If you can see it clearly, it's because some part of you knows it. The moment you judge it, you've touched it.

That doesn't mean you *are* it, but it does mean it's yours to look at.

That's the real journey: Noticing when it's happening, catching yourself in the projection before you turn it into a story about them. We all do it; we project what we haven't fully claimed. We judge what we've secretly struggled with. We resent in others what we haven't forgiven in ourselves. That's not a character flaw. It's not shameful. It's just human.

But it's also your most powerful teacher, if you're willing to own it. And to show you what that looks like in real life, let me introduce you to someone who did exactly that.

SARAH'S STORY: FROM FRUSTRATION TO FLOW (AT WORK AND HOME)

Sarah was one of those high-performing managers who got things done. Her team knew her as a powerhouse, organized, efficient, and relentless. But there was one employee, Mike, who drove her up the wall. He needed constant hand-holding, repeated instructions, and reassurance on even the smallest tasks.

Sarah came into coaching pissed. "He just doesn't get it. I've explained it 100 times." Instead of agreeing, I asked her the real question: "Sarah, what if what you're seeing in Mike is actually a reflection of something within yourself? What might that be?" Cue the eye roll. Long silence. She wasn't feeling it. Eventually, Sarah agreed to try something different, a three-part challenge I called STOP, STEP-IN, STAY.

STOP: IDENTIFYING THE REAL ISSUE

The next time Mike asked for help, Sarah paused and asked herself:

- What's triggering me right now?
- Is it his neediness . . . or my belief that people should "just get it"?
- What feeling is this bringing up? Impatience? Frustration? Superiority?

And it hit her. That same irritation? She felt it at home with her kids. Her eight-year-old daughter constantly asked for help. Her son needed reminders every ten minutes. She always swooped in and did it for them. She realized she wasn't just frustrated with Mike or her children; she was frustrated by her own unconscious belief that *asking for help equals weakness.*

71

STEP-IN: EMBRACING CURIOSITY AND COMPASSION

This time, she got curious:

- What is this frustration trying to teach me?
- How am I participating in this dynamic?
- Am I projecting my perfectionism onto other people?

The answers were uncomfortable, but freeing. Sarah journaled. She reflected. She owned it. "I built my whole life around being the one who figured it out. I didn't just expect excellence, I demanded it . . . because I never felt like I could afford to struggle." She fully stepped into her truth.

STAY: SITTING WITH THE DISCOMFORT AND TAKING ACTION

This part? The hardest. Instead of fixing, correcting, or rescuing, Sarah stayed with it. She let Mike solve his own problems. She let her daughter try first. She let her son stumble through.

She didn't swoop in. And guess what? They stepped up.

At work, Mike began offering solutions instead of waiting for answers. At home, her kids started taking initiative. And Sarah? She finally stopped feeling like the damn Google of her family and team members. She found relief, not just results. Sarah's world shifted, not because Mike changed, but because she did. Her mornings got lighter. Her team became more confident. Her home felt calmer. And for the first time in years, she felt like she could *breathe*.

That's what happens when you flip the mirror and own the reflection. That's what happens when you stop outsourcing your triggers and start reclaiming your patterns. That's what happens when you take ownership, expand, and learn from your own triggers.

THOUGHT SHIFTER

The STOP, STEP-IN, STAY Challenge

Feeling triggered by someone? Here's your call-in moment.

STOP

When the judgment flares up, pause. Get honest.

- What am I seeing in them that annoys me?
- What feelings are coming up?
- Where else is this showing up in my life?

_____

_____

_____

_____

_____

_____

_____

STEP-IN

Get curious—not defensive.

- What is this experience trying to teach me?
- Am I contributing to this pattern?
- Am I projecting something I haven't healed?

_____

_____

_____

_____

_____

_____

_____

_____

STAY

Sit with the discomfort and take aligned action.

- What lesson am I resisting?
- How can I reframe this for growth?
- What's one action I can take to shift this pattern today?

_____

_____

_____

_____

_____

_____

_____

You don't need to fix it all today. You just need to start seeing clearly. And that starts in the mirror. No mask. No filter. No deflection. No shame. Just truth. Just awareness. Just: **"I see me."**

CHAPTER 4

· · · · · · · · ·

WHEN AWARENESS
WRECKS YOUR RELATIONSHIPS
(AND SETS YOU FREE)

A NEW WAY TO SEE IT, THE COURAGE TO
LET GO, AND THE FREEDOM TO GROW—
THE CHOICE IS YOURS

Relationships are a part of life. Period. There are layers, types, and complexities—from casual acquaintances to soul-deep, ride-or-die commitments. Some feel easy. Some are exhausting. Some we crave. Some we endure. And some? Some we walk away from, burning the damn bridge with zero regret.

Let me open the door wider for you:

"I'm done."

"I don't need anyone."

"I can do this on my own."

"Cross me and you're out."

"I'll check you off and push you aside in a second."

Yep. That was me. That was my defense system. My badge of self-protection. The armor I wrapped myself in to stay sharp, survive, and lead my life. The moment someone crossed that final line? You got my backside as your new view, because I was walking away, maybe even running. And honestly? Some of those exits? Damn right, I'd do them again. Probably faster.

But here's where everything shifted . . .

What happens when you stop defending and start getting curious about the pattern? What if there's a deeper reason certain relationships crack, fade, or explode when you grow? What if your relationships are a living, breathing mirror—not of your worth, but of your awareness?

There's a saying I heard a lot growing up: "Relationships are the fabric of our lives."

But are they? Think about it . . . are they the fabric or the thread? What really keeps us warm? Just something to ponder. Maybe they're all of it. But here's what I know for sure: You can't outrun relationships. You never will. You can disappear to a mountaintop, hide away on some off-grid island. And guess what? You'd still have a relationship. With your surroundings. With your energy. With your choices. With you. There's no escaping relationships. It's only how aware you are of them. Let me make one thing clear before we dive in. You're not getting a fluffy how-to guide to perfect relationships wrapped in fake positivity. You won't get that from me. What you *will* get? A perspective that challenges your beliefs. A chapter designed to crack you wide open, to help you question, unpack, and rewrite the rules so you can actually thrive in your relationships with others. And most importantly? With yourself. Some relationships stay. Some go. Some stretch you. Some suffocate you. And some? Some carry the exact lesson you didn't know you needed until you finally listened.

It wasn't a normal session. This is part of my monthly non-negotiable—a sound bath, my reset, my ritual for realignment with myself. I don't just coach this; I live it. But I didn't walk in to relax. I went for clarity. For release. For truth. And wow, did I get it.

It had been one of those weeks where relationship chaos was swirling: my life, my clients' lives, and my personal world. Misalignment everywhere. The questions were hitting hard in my head, and the fight to not run, but to choose differently, was kick-ass hard.

I kept asking myself the harder questions, trying to quiet the chatter, trying to override the old "done" reel looping in my mind. What do you do when your growth triggers resistance in the people closest to you? How do you honor your expansion when others want you to stay small, stay the same? Why does stepping into your power sometimes feel like an eviction notice to the people you love?

I could feel it in my body, the tension of trying to grow while still carrying people who weren't walking their own path. And then came the whisper.

"Wash your feet."

I said it out loud to Stephanie, my therapist. "You're gonna think I'm crazy, but I feel like I'm supposed to wash my feet before we start." She looked at me, jaw practically on the floor, then pointed to a sound bowl at my feet. "You're not crazy. I just bought this standing sound bath bowl this week, and now I know—it's for you. I had no clue why I was so strongly nudged to purchase it."

We both laughed because when you're dialed in, the universe doesn't play subtle. I stepped in, and that's when everything started to crack open. The vibration hit from the soles of my feet to the top of my head. Everything shifted.

THE DOWNLOAD THAT HIT MY SOUL

The message came fast, clear, and deep. I was lying on the table, and Stephanie was at my feet. The second she touched them, I heard it, loud inside me, out of nowhere.

"Where you walk, they will walk."

She moved to my knees.

"Where you kneel, they will kneel."

Then my hips.

"Where you stand, they will stand."

Finally, my shoulders and back started buzzing with energy and tenderness. And then came the full message. The part that cracked me wide open.

"Life is full of relationships. Some will walk with you. Some will kneel with you. Some, you will shoulder. And some . . . they'll try to climb on your back so you can carry them."

That last line hit me straight in my gut. Because let's be honest, sometimes you're not overwhelmed because you're doing too much. You're overwhelmed because you're carrying too many people who refuse to walk their own path.

THE FOUR FREQUENCIES OF RELATIONSHIP

That experience gave me exactly what I came for: clarity. The kind of clarity that doesn't just land in your mind but hits your body, your energy, your knowing.

I saw the pattern. I saw the truth. And I saw the real reason so many of us stay stuck, overwhelmed, or weighed down by the relationships around us. It all comes back to what I now refer to as the Four Frequencies of Relationship. Every connection you have falls into one of these categories. Some expand you. Some stretch you. Some hold you steady. And some? Some drain the life right out of you.

It's time to name them with bold, unapologetic clarity. Because the moment you step into real awareness, you finally see your relationships for what they are . . . and what they're not. That's the moment everything shifts. You get to choose differently. You get to decide what you want more of and what you're done carrying.

When you're clear, you can see exactly what your relationships are expanding in your life. Are you expanding ease, exhaustion, alignment, chaos, community, control, or something else entirely? Seeing it is the awareness. Awareness is your power to choose. And you can't choose what you can't or refuse to see.

The second you start calling your relationships what they truly are, you reclaim your energy, your growth, and your freedom. You set the rules. You call the shots. You decide what stays, what goes, and what fuels your next level.

Alright then, let's go!

1. The Walkers

These are your people. You grow together. You challenge each other. You evolve. There's momentum here. Step for step, stride for stride. No dragging. No performing. Just real, aligned growth—the kind of expansion that stretches possibility, not just your comfort zone.

2. The Kneelers

Your sacred-space people. The ones who show up for the quiet moments of truth, the stillness, the grief, the prayers, the depth, the joy. The moments that don't need fixing, only witnessing and presence. They may not always walk beside you, but when it's time to kneel? They're right there.

3. The Shouldered

The ones you've lifted. Encouraged. Held steady when life hit hard. The ones who leaned on your strength, for a moment, a season, or a stretch of the journey. But here's what makes the shoulder space tricky: It can feel good, even rewarding, at first. You tell yourself you're being supportive, that you're strong enough to carry them, that they just need time. And maybe they do.

But stay there too long, and the shoulder stops being a healthy support; it becomes a trap, because the shoulder is meant to be temporary. A place for encouragement, not dependence. The longer they stay? The more your energy leaks. The more your boundaries blur. The more you start carrying weight that isn't yours and calling it love.

And when that happens? You're the one who feels trapped, drained, and disconnected from your own alignment.

If they never stand, never walk, never kneel beside you again, that's on them. That's their choice, their work, their path. But here's your part: It's on you to stay whole. To stay healthy, emotionally, physically, and mentally. To stop carrying what was never yours to hold forever.

You've got the wisdom. Use it. Check your alignment, your energy, and your reason for keeping them there.

4. The Riders (The Back Crowd)

Whew. These are the ones who climb on your back, not to grow, but to ride your life instead of building their own. They weigh you down. On your back, they appear bigger. They feel stronger. Meanwhile, in your exhaustion, you start shrinking just trying to keep them comfortable and trying to keep them from falling off. You carry them. Make excuses for them. Drain your energy keeping them afloat. All the while? You lose your balance. You lose your voice. You lose your momentum.

CLAIMING YOUR NEW RELATIONSHIP RULES

I want to share something with you—just in case no one's ever told you. Most of us haven't heard this clearly enough, but it's time you did. The relationships that drain you? The ones weighing on your back, throwing off your balance, leaking your energy?

You let them on.

You let them stay.

But here's the good part: You get to choose differently. You get to shift this. You get to decide who walks with you, who kneels with you, and who's no longer riding on your back.

Here's how you take your power back:

Step 1: Name What No Longer Resonates

Say it out loud with no guilt, no filter.

"Who or what feels heavy?"

"Where are you over-functioning just to keep the peace?"

"What relationship feels like duty instead of desire?"

Naming it doesn't make you cruel. It makes you conscious. It makes you powerful.

Step 2: Own Your Part

They climbed on, but you opened the door.

You carried them to feel needed, liked, safe, or in control. No shame in that. But once you're aware of it? Everything changes.

Ask yourself:

"Where did I say yes to keep the peace and avoid being judged?"

"What role did I play in keeping this dynamic alive?"

Awareness without ownership is just observation. Ownership? That's where your power lives.

Step 3: Separate Care from Carrying

Repeat after me: "I can care for people and still choose myself."

Love doesn't require exhaustion. Boundaries aren't betrayal. You don't have to carry people to prove your loyalty, your love, or your strength. If your worth is tied to how much you carry others? It's time to rewrite that contract. You can love people without sacrificing your peace, your wellness, or your alignment. You can support them without breaking yourself.

Step 4: Claim Your New Alignment

You're not going back to who you were. That version served you then— but you've outgrown that now.

Ask yourself:

- Who am I becoming?
- What does this next level require of me?
- Where does my energy say YES? And where does it scream NO?

Claim your alignment. Stand in it. Walk in it. Kneel in it. But stop carrying what weighs you down.

THOUGHT SHIFTER

Your Relationship Alignment Check

Grab your journal, your notes app, whatever works.

Reflect with fire and honesty:

1. Who am I still carrying that no longer belongs on my back?

_____

_____

_____

_____

_____

2. What am I afraid to lose if I set them down?

_____

_____

_____

_____

_____

_____

3. Where am I kneeling or walking while still shouldering unnecessary weight?

_____

_____

_____

_____

_____

_____

4. What relationship dynamic feels outdated?

_____

_____

_____

_____

_____

_____

5. What does claiming my new alignment look like in action?

You don't have to blow it all up.

You don't need to perform your boundaries for applause.

But you *do* get to choose—when you're ready.

Because your next expansion? It's waiting on you to get honest, get aligned, and get free.

CHAPTER 5

· · · · · · · · ·

FOUNDATIONAL FACTS
THE SCIENCE OF EXPANSION

Let's get one thing straight: Your brain is powerful. But most of the time? It's not focused on making you successful, happy, or fulfilled. It's focused on keeping you safe, or at least what it believes is safe. But "safe" doesn't always mean aligned. Sometimes it just means familiar.

Your brain is a pattern-reinforcing machine. And its number one job? Efficiency. It wants to conserve energy. So the moment you experience something more than once, a thought, a reaction, a belief, a habit, your brain codes it into a shortcut. A default. A groove. You think it's just "how you are." But often, it's just how you've been repeating.

Here's the scientific term: **Neuroplasticity**. Your brain is literally moldable. It strengthens the neural pathways you use the most.

- Practice self-doubt? It becomes a superhighway.
- Feed it fear? It builds a fortress.
- Train it in truth, courage, and curiosity? It starts rewiring.

You are always reinforcing something. And expansion? That's about doing it on purpose.

You might remember back in Agreement 1 when we first talked about your reticular activating system (RAS), your brain's filter, your

Expansion GPS. We cracked open the door then because it's that important to your daily experience. But understanding how your RAS works isn't just a fun science fact—it's a core expansion factor. Because you can't consciously expand what you don't consciously rewire. And now that you've been building your awareness, it's time to take it further. You're not just noticing your filter anymore. You're about to update it.

The reticular activating system is the filter in your brainstem that decides what information gets your attention and what doesn't. Imagine your RAS as your brain's VIP bouncer. It only lets in what matches the list. And what's the list made of? Your beliefs.

Your thoughts. Your expectations.

- If you believe the world is against you, your RAS filters for rejection and obstacles.
- If you believe you're not good enough, your RAS highlights every mistake and overlooks every win.
- If you believe you're powerful and expanding, your RAS scans for opportunities, alignment, and evidence of growth.

Your reality reflects your RAS. But your RAS reflects your inner reality. So, if you want to change what you see? You've got to change what you believe.

THOUGHT REHEARSAL: WIRING YOUR FUTURE ON PURPOSE

Your brain doesn't actually know the difference between something real and something vividly imagined if you engage emotionally with it.

So, when you replay a failure or spiral into worst-case scenarios? Your brain stores that like practice.

But guess what?

You can use that same exact wiring system to create expansion instead.

- Visualize speaking with confidence? Your brain starts building that pathway.
- Practice gratitude for a future that hasn't arrived yet? Your body starts aligning with it.
- Declare a truth with emotional energy? Your RAS updates the filter.

You're not just "imagining." You're installing. Here is the real version to replace that old "fake it till you make it" phrase? This is the real version: **"Wire it till you live it."**

No shame. No "Why can't I just change?" Your brain isn't broken. It's been practicing patterns that no longer serve you. And now, you're about to practice new ones.

JENNA, THE RED CARS, AND THE RAS RESET

Jenna came into our session barely holding it together. She had just gone through a breakup, and everything felt heavy. Her energy was flat, her voice distant, and her words? On repeat: "I just keep attracting the same kind of people. Same patterns. Same heartbreak." She wasn't wrong, but her brain was running old wiring: "This is just how it is for me."

I didn't give her a journal prompt or assign a mindset mantra. I looked her straight in the eye and said, "I want you to do one thing this week. It's called the Red Car Exercise."

She blinked. "Seriously? What's that gonna do?"

"Start looking for red cars. Everywhere. That's it. No fixing. No forcing. Just looking."

Skeptical but willing, Jenna tried it. And sure enough, they started popping up. At the grocery store. At the gas station. On the freeway. She didn't realize that the red cars had always been there. Her brain just hadn't been tuned to see them.

Her RAS had been filtering for sadness, rejection, and stuckness. But when she tuned her focus, even neutrally, her brain started catching something new. And once that door cracked open?

Jenna realized: If she could retrain her brain to find red cars . . . she could retrain it to find:

- Joy
- Proof she was growing
- Signs she was okay
- Opportunities for connection
- People who smiled back

When she returned the next week, something had shifted. Her energy was lighter. Her tone was more curious. Her face? Unclouded. "You're not going to believe this," she said. "I actually felt . . . playful again."

That's when I slid a small bag across the table and said: "These are my Be With Words cards.

Pick a word as often as you want and look for it. Live into it. Expand into it."

She exhaled, long, deep, free.

What you focus on expands.

What you seek, you strengthen.

What you wire, you live.

You're constantly wiring something. You're not stuck with how you were shaped. You're not fixed, final, or finished. You're wiring yourself, right now, through your choices, thoughts, emotional focus, and daily repetitions. This is what real expansion looks like: not sudden epiphanies, but small, practiced pivots, over and over, until the future you want becomes the life you're living.

You're either rehearsing your past or rehearsing your power. Choose wisely.

THOUGHT SHIFTER

Choose Your Frequency

Pull out your journal or just pause and reflect deeply:

1. What are three thoughts I repeat often that reinforce limitation or fear?

_____

_____

_____

_____

_____

2. What do those thoughts train my brain to look for or expect?

_____

_____

_____

_____

_____

3. What is one new belief I'm ready to install—even if it feels new or uncomfortable?

_____

_____

_____

_____

_____

4. How can I rehearse that belief daily (through visualization, declaration, or action)?

_____

_____

_____

_____

_____

5. What's one moment I can interrupt an old pattern and install a new one today?

_____

_____

_____

_____

_____

Be With Words Bonus:

Choose a "word" for the week. Look for it on purpose. Speak it. Feel it. BE it. Anchor into it.

Because what you focus on expands. And what you install with intention becomes who you are.

Expansion doesn't happen because you learn something new. Expansion locks in because you **choose** to see, believe, and rehearse it until it becomes you. You're not just noticing anymore. You're becoming the one who rewires, on purpose.

. . . .

CHAPTER 6

THE ENERGY STAIRCASE— YOUR EXPANSION GPS

EXPANSION HAS A FREQUENCY. AND SO DO YOU.

Whether you realize it or not, you're operating at a certain energetic level—a vibe, a tone, and a presence that shapes how you think, feel, and experience others.

Some days you're magnetic. Clear. Grounded. You walk in, and the whole room shifts.

Other days? You're spiraling in doubt, control, or people-pleasing, wondering why everything feels so damn hard. That's not random. That's energy. Energy isn't something you just have: It's something you manage, choose, and expand.

We've been taught to focus on actions, outcomes, and behavior. But what is the real driver underneath all of that? Your energy. Your energy awareness changes everything. Your energy is what fuels your tone, presence, communication, leadership, choices, and vibe. Awareness is your power to choose, and without it, you don't even know you have a choice.

When you're not saying a word, your energy is still speaking. So if you want to shift what's happening in your life, whether it's how you lead, how you love, or how you show up, you need to start by tuning in to the frequency you're living in.

A FRAMEWORK I USE WITH CLIENTS: THE ENERGY STAIRCASE

One of the tools I use when coaching individuals and teams is what I call the Energy Staircase. It's not a model I created from scratch; it's inspired by neuroscience, energy work, and my years of personal and professional growth. What I've done is turn it into something relatable, teachable, and coachable in the real world.

Think of it like this: Your energy lives somewhere on a staircase, from low, draining, reactive states . . . to higher, aligned, responsive, power-FULL ones. You're not one level. You're in motion all the time—up, down, and across—sometimes by default; sometimes by choice.

What I help people do is recognize their baseline, spot their patterns, and learn how to shift their frequency on purpose. This is where we stop letting our triggers zap us and stress run the show and where we start leading from alignment and purpose.

Each energetic "step" reflects a certain state you might be living in:

- Low-energy steps feel like blame, blowups, burnout, apathy, control, or overreaction.
- Mid-range energy often shows up as people-pleasing, over-functioning, judging, or tolerating things that don't work.
- Higher steps feel like presence, curiosity, creativity, clarity, and deep connection.

There's no "perfect step." All steps have their advantages and disadvantages. You simply move up and down all day. The key is: Can you name where you are? Can you shift when it's time?

ENERGY PRECEDES OUTCOME

To make this more realistic for you, have you ever:

- Walked into a room where everything looked fine . . . but the vibe was just off?
- Said the "right" words, but the energy behind them fell flat or stirred conflict?
- Made a smart decision on paper that felt heavy in your body?

That's energy. And it's why we can't just think our way to better outcomes. We have to tune our way forward.

Let's say you catch yourself reacting, snapping, controlling, blaming, or shutting down. That's a cue: You're hanging out on a lower step.

Instead of judging yourself, try this:

- Pause.
- Breathe.
- Ask: "What am I actually afraid of here?"
- Ask: "What's one step up I could shift into?"
- Reframe with curiosity or compassion.

This is not about faking positivity. It's about creating energetic congruence, about choosing a frequency that feels more aligned and powerful for who you want to be.

MAYA'S STAIRCASE MOMENT

Maya was part of her company's HR and people team. We all know her; she is the one who keeps things "human," clear, and collaborative. She was known for being efficient, high-performing, and always ready with a policy or plan.

But lately? Everything felt like it was slipping sideways.

Her calendar was packed, and her brain was fried. She was short with her coworkers, and people started "checking her mood" before giving her updates. One of the new hires even asked another team member, "Hey . . . is she always like this?"

At home, her daughter stopped asking for help with schoolwork. Her partner walked on eggshells. And Maya kept thinking: "Why am I the only one who sees how urgent everything is?"

That's what Step 2 energy sounds like. Protective. Reactive. Controlling in the name of being helpful.

She came into a session with me and said, "I don't understand, I'm doing everything I'm supposed to do."

So I pulled out the Energy Staircase and walked her through it.

She blinked. Smirked. Exhaled.

"So . . . I've basically been camped out on Step 2." We laughed. But she got it. Fast. She saw how she'd been showing up as the fixer, the fire extinguisher, the emotional bouncer, and how her team, her home, and her nervous system were paying the price.

"I thought I was being strong," she said. "But I've just been… tight."

We didn't overhaul her overnight.

We picked one moment, one pattern, one energetic shift at a time.

- When someone brought her a problem, she paused before replying.
- When her daughter asked for help, she softened her tone first.
- When a colleague made a mistake, she didn't react or take over. She responded with support, giving them space to learn, correct it, and grow. Instead of rescuing, she started asking:

"How can I support you in making this right?"

She stopped trying to micromanage outcomes and started managing her energy.

After two weeks, her team started asking her opinion more, not just about compliance, but culture. One coworker said, "You've felt different lately. It's like . . . you're still you, but calmer."

At home, her daughter began asking questions again. Her partner started talking without fear of a reaction.

Maya's expansion didn't come from mastering the staircase. It came from realizing she'd been camped out on a lower step and choosing, one breath at a time, to climb up.

That's leadership. That's embodiment. And that's how you shift everything—not by pushing harder, but by vibrating higher.

Want to go deeper with this? This framework is just a glimpse. When I work with clients and teams, we go deeper into the roots, the patterns, the default responses, and the opportunities for recalibration. Because once you know what step you're standing on and why . . . everything changes.

If this stirred something in you, bookmark this chapter. Come back to it.

Let it land in layers. And when you're ready? Reach out. We've got deeper work to do.

THOUGHT SHIFTER

Where Are You Now?

Remember when we talked about how energy leads before words do back in Chapter 2? Here's where we take that even further. This is your real-time gut check. When things feel off, stuck, heavy, or chaotic, pause and ask:

1. What step of energy have I been operating from most often this week?

_____

_____

_____

_____

_____

2. What thoughts or habits are reinforcing that level?

_____

_____

_____

_____

_____

3. What's the cost of staying in that energy?

_____

_____

_____

_____

_____

4. What step would serve me more powerfully right now?

_____

_____

_____

_____

_____

5. What's one breath, one choice, or one shift that would move me toward it?

_____

_____

_____

_____

_____

You don't have to move from stuck to enlightened in a single leap. Just take the next step up. One breath. One recalibration. One energetic shift at a time. That's not fluff; that's expansion.

CHAPTER 7

• • • • • • • • • •

THE SPACE BETWEEN WHO YOU'VE BEEN AND WHO YOU'RE BECOMING

This isn't the end. This is the in-between. And the in-between? It's where your power lives. You've already begun expanding; that was clear the moment you opened this book. You've met your patterns. You've met your resistance. You've met your power. And now you're standing in what I call the space between. That space is gritty. It's where the old you starts to unravel, but the new you isn't quite locked in yet. It's not where things are fully clear, but where you start getting honest. It's where you stop performing, start aligning, and begin creating from intention instead of habit.

And if you're feeling messy right now? Good. That's the point. Growth isn't a straight line; it's a stretch. When's the most tense moment you pull a rubber band to launch it? Right before it snaps forward. That tension? That's where most people quit. They backpedal into safety. They go silent. They pretend the expansion didn't matter. But you? If you've made it this far, you're not here to snap back. You're here to **stretch with purpose**. To breathe into the tension. To keep choosing forward, even when everything old inside you whispers "go back."

The space between who you've been and who you're becoming? It's sacred. It's sweaty. It's not polished, but it's **real**. "Clarity" is often a lie we chase when we're uncomfortable. We say we need a plan. A timeline. A perfect roadmap. You don't need to have it all figured out. What we need is permission. To shift. To explore. To not know.

I'm going to offer you some truths I've learned in my own expansion and from the brave humans I've coached through theirs:

- You can feel doubt and still choose power.
- You can want more and still love what you have.
- You can expand without a plan.
- You can honor who you've been while becoming someone new.
- You can move even if you're scared.

You're not here to get it perfect. You're here to get it aligned.

Before we close this section, I want you to pause. There is power in the pause we allow ourselves. Don't rush into the next part of the book. Don't fast-forward into leadership or love without taking inventory of the life you're leading right now.

Sit with these questions:

- What have I learned about myself in this process so far?
- What beliefs or patterns have already started to shift?
- Where am I still clinging to an outdated version of myself?
- What's calling me forward?

This is the space between. And honoring this space? That's the mark of someone who's not just talking about expansion, but is living it. You don't need to wait until you've "arrived." You're already becoming. With every honest journal entry. With every recalibrated breath. With every moment you say, "Wait . . . that's not how I want to show up," and choose again. The space between who you've been and who you're becoming is full of gold—if you're willing to stay long enough to mine it.

THOUGHT SHIFTER

Honor the In-Between

Let this moment land. Take five to ten minutes to be honest with yourself.

1. Who am I no longer willing to be?

_____

_____

_____

_____

_____

_____

_____

2. What patterns am I leaving behind, even if they're still tempting?

_____

_____

_____

_____

_____

_____

_____

3. What energy, values, or truths am I stepping into more fully?

_____

_____

_____

_____

_____

_____

_____

_____

4. What part of me is still scared? What part of me is ready to lead?

_____

_____

_____

_____

_____

_____

_____

_____

_____

5. What will I choose to expand in this next season?

_____

_____

_____

_____

_____

_____

_____

_____

_____

Your not at the finish line. It's a threshold. And you, my friend, are ready.

FACTOR 2

· · · · · · · · ·

EXPAND IN LEADERSHIP

HOW YOU SHOW UP

If you've made it this far, or if you skipped around (no shame; I do it too), there are a few truths you need to carry into this next section. First, the core theme of this entire book experience:

You are constantly expanding something. Whether you're aware of it or not, your energy, beliefs, and habits create ripples. Second, and this one's a game-changer: Your emotions and triggers aren't the problem. They're the message. They're your portal. They show you where the next expansion is begging to break through.

At the start of this journey, I asked you to make three foundational agreements with yourself:

1. You're already expanding something, so let's get intentional about what.
2. Life is a series of choices, and every choice expands something.
3. Alignment starts by knowing what matters most to *you*.

Now it's time to take those agreements off the page and into the world. Into your work. Your team. Your conversations. Your presence. Leadership is about the energy, intention, and purpose you bring into every room you walk into. In this level of leadership, there are no titles. Leadership is the ripple you create, whether you're in a boardroom, a video call, or wiping peanut butter off the counter at home. You're always leading something: yourself, your energy, your reactions, your choices.

So here's where I say. Ask yourself this:

What's your energy saying before you speak?

What's your leadership teaching when you're not talking?

Because if they're not doing it . . . They're not seeing it. And what they're seeing . . . is *you*.

Expanding leadership starts right here. It's not about more pressure or more tasks, it's about deeper alignment, greater presence, and real-time integrity.

In this factor, you'll explore:

- How to lead from alignment instead of authority
- How to create cultures where accountability, feedback, and follow up aren't feared, but are fuel
- How to shift from control and compliance to curiosity and collaboration
- How to move from managing outcomes to expanding humans
- How to stay anchored in your energy, even when chaos swirls

Presence is the move. Not image. Not perfection. Not performance. Presence. The kind that doesn't posture, pretend, or perfect. The kind that holds the room, the moment, the mirror, and says: *"Let's go. We got this. You got this."* Being real? That's the power play. Perfection will drain you. Performing will betray you. Trying to "get it right"? That'll shrink you. Leadership is **integrity in motion;** it's what people *feel* before you say a word. It's self-awareness that builds trust. The energy people lean toward, not away from. When alignment clicks inside, expansion flows outside. Leadership stops being a role you perform and becomes a ripple you lead with.

Now it's time to ponder this one . . . **What would it feel like to lead from who you are, not just what you do?** That's what we're unlocking in this section. We're pulling back the curtain and going there. When you do the work by fully stepping into each chapter:

You'll get clear on the difference between boss energy and true leadership presence.

You'll redefine accountability as empowerment, not punishment.

You'll discover why follow up is the heartbeat of trust.

And you'll step into whole-self leadership not as a luxury, but as your secret edge.

Whether you lead one or one thousand, you are expanding a culture. Is the culture you're leading right now something you'd be proud to multiply? Or is it one you've been unconsciously reinforcing out of habit, fear, or autopilot? If it's not where you want it yet, that's good. That means you're awake. And if it is? Buckle up because we're about to go deeper.

CHAPTER 8

WHOLE-SELF LEADERSHIP

LEAD FROM THE INSIDE OUT

Let's be honest: Leadership programs are everywhere. But transformation? That's rare.

Most leadership training fails because it teaches surface-level skills and completely ignores the real source of leadership, *you*. Your mind. Your emotions. Your energy. Your beliefs. Your soul.

Here's the truth most people miss: If your beliefs don't change, your energy won't change. Your emotions won't shift. Your behavior won't stick. Skills without belief work? Temporary at best. The work is integrating that source into how you lead, how you show up, how you influence. Because leadership isn't just skill—it's alignment in action. This chapter is the heartbeat of your leadership. It's the foundation of how we lead differently. Boldly. Wholly.

We call it whole-self leadership. You'll learn to claim it and own it right here. Whole-self leadership means you're leading from alignment and not from a script. It's the kind of leadership that doesn't fizzle after a motivational keynote or fade once the workbook closes. It's the kind that *sticks* and goes in deep because it's wired into what you believe, how you think, how you show up, and how you influence everything around you. **Whole-self leadership is the future of leadership, and**

it's nothing like the past. It's about expanding your leadership from the inside out, rooted in your own clarity, energy, truth, and purpose. It's not about checking training boxes, memorizing competency models, or showing up as the most polished person in the room. Here's how we define it:

Whole-self leadership = mind + emotion + energy + soul.

We integrate these four core dimensions:

- **Mind:** Your beliefs, thoughts, and mindset. Break free from old beliefs about what a leader "should" be and lead from who you *are*, from your identity.
- **Emotions:** Your capacity to feel, regulate, and connect
- **Energy:** Your awareness of how you shift space without speaking
- **Soul:** That's the part of you that knows why you're here and what matters most. You lead from values, purpose, and connection—not from fear, control, or trying to prove energy.

When you lead from your whole self, all four layers, you're not just guiding people. You're *expanding* them to do the same. This is no longer about soft skills. This is *your leading edge,* your differentiator. And when you lead from your whole self, you shift cultures. You create ripples. You build belief because your people *feel* you before they follow you. You don't just shift meetings, drive results, or get buy-in. You get to shift the entire place from the inside out. We're not just talking about a new model. We're flipping the entire conversation around leadership on its head.

If your leadership isn't rooted in the whole of who you are, it's just performance. And performance exhausts people. But presence? Presence empowers them. And the only way you can lead from presence . . . is by leading from your *whole self.*

Whole-self leadership is the core of everything I teach. It's not fluff. It's not "woo." And it's definitely not optional if you want to be the kind of leader who creates real impact, not just productivity. Whole-self leadership is grounded in this truth: *Your people can't rise higher than the version of you they're following. If you don't like what they're doing, ask what they're seeing. You're the ceiling. So rise . . . or watch them hit their heads on your limits.*

Let that sink in for a second. You can't delegate trust if you don't trust your own voice. You can't cultivate resilience if you're stuck in survival mode. You can't hold space for others if you don't know how to return to your own. Most leaders have been trained to override themselves. To bulldoze their truth. To smile through the burnout and call it "showing up." To push through. Stay polished. Look productive. Deliver results, check the boxes, shake hands, and lead the meetings. To be the strategy and do the doing while directing everyone else to perform at their peak even when you're running on fumes. Don't feel. Don't flinch. Don't slow down. Just grit your teeth, slap on your leadership face, and pretend you're fine.

And for the ones who really do care and are trying to lead differently than the poor leaders they survived? They armor up with the best intentions. They overcompensate, over-function, and carry the whole damn load thinking that's what good leadership looks like. They try to be everything for everyone and then wonder why they feel like an impostor, why they're exhausted, and why no one else seems to lead like they do. Here's where the whole damn thing flips: The team isn't failing. The team is following. They're just mirroring what's modeled. And doing exactly what's been allowed. That's why so many teams disengage—not because the leader is weak, but because the leader has been busy doing it *all* instead of leading what actually matters.

You're not a machine. You're a human. And humans expand based on energy, not just effort. Whole-self leadership is not a perk. It's your dang *edge*. It's how you expand sustainably instead of burning out. It's how you build trust, not just systems. It's how you stop managing people . . . and actually *lead* from your whole self at all times.

Let me show you what I mean. A while back, I was in a gas station convenience store, which was not exactly a sacred temple of leadership, right? You know the kind: fluorescent lights buzzing, coffee burnt, snacks calling your name. I'd had a long day, and all I wanted was to grab what I needed and go. The cashier? Clearly *over it*. Flat tone. Zero eye contact. One-word answers. Her whole vibe screamed, "Let's just get this over with!" I could feel my own irritation rising. My body was matching her energy before I even said a word. I was about to throw my own mini attitude right back, short, clipped, done. But then I caught myself. That moment? *That* was leadership. Leadership is how your energy walks into a room, any room. It's how you hold yourself when someone else's energy is off. It's the choice to influence instead of absorb. So I shifted. I made eye contact. I smiled. I asked her, genuinely, how her day was going, not to be polite, but to connect. And you know what? She softened. Her shoulders dropped. She looked up. She smiled back. And then she *thanked me*. Not just for asking.

But for actually *seeing her*. I'll never forget what she told me: "No one from here has even asked how I'm doing, not even my boss. You're the first person all day who's talked to me like I mattered." That landed with me and landed hard, and why will you hear me say this all the time? You're **always leading something**, even if it's just the energy of a ninety-second interaction in a gas station. You're expanding something with every choice, every breath, every response.

That day, I wasn't leading a team. I was leading a moment. And it mattered.

Leadership isn't just about guiding others; it's about aligning our actions, decisions, and energy with our core values and the needs of our teams and all whom we come in contact with. Just as we seek balance in life, we must seek alignment in leadership. This is about achieving balance and harmony in all aspects of life, including leadership.

Here's what I see consistently: leaders who are excellent *technically*, but disconnected *energetically*. They've been trained in strategy, but not in presence. They've been told to manage results, but not relationships. They have tools . . . but no trust in themselves or in their people.

MEET DAVID

David was one of those leaders who looked like he had it all dialed in. He was sharp, respected, results-driven, and deeply committed to his team. The kind of guy who'd say yes before you finished asking. On paper? A solid A+. In the hallway? All business. On the inside? Fried.

When we started working together, David wasn't in crisis, but he *was* on autopilot. Leading from the neck up. Strategy? Locked in. KPIs? On track. Presence? Nowhere to be found. He was operating through the motions, mentally sharp but emotionally unavailable. His default mode was hustle, a badge of honor and a blind spot rolled into one.

I introduced him to the Leadership Wheel, a tool I use to help leaders assess their alignment across key areas like communication, emotional intelligence, vision, follow through, and more. David took it seriously, but let me be clear: *He thought he was crushing it.* And then . . . he did something I didn't expect. Without me suggesting it, David brought the tool to his team. He handed them the wheel and asked them to rate him. All eight spokes. No filter. No anonymity. Just full-out, open feedback. He was convinced the results would confirm what he already believed, that he was a strong, engaged leader doing his best for his people. But that's not what came back. His team didn't attack him. They didn't roast him. But they *did* tell the truth.

They saw him as "too busy" to connect.

They felt like he listened to problems but didn't follow through.

They described him as high-functioning . . . but emotionally checked out.

They said his energy didn't feel safe for feedback because he was always rushing to the next thing.

David was stunned. And to his credit, he didn't spiral. He didn't defend. He didn't crumble.

He owned it. He looked at me and said, "I thought I was being a good leader . . . because I've been working my ass off for them. But now I see I've been leading from effort, not energy. From task, not presence."

And that's when the shift happened. David stopped leading just from strategy and started leading from self-awareness. He restructured his calendar to include intentional one-on-ones that focused on energy, accountability, and development—not just metrics. He built weekly rituals where team members could check in on how they were doing *as humans*. He stopped outsourcing emotional connection to HR and made it part of his job because he finally understood it *was* his job.

Six months later, in his weekly team huddle, his team voluntarily asked to do the Wheel again.

And this time? They didn't just say *he* had changed; they said *they* had changed. They felt seen. Valued. Trusted. They were showing up more boldly because *he* had stopped playing small with his presence. That's the ripple of **whole-self leadership**. When one person commits to "growing forward" and expanding, everyone feels it.

YOUR TURN: THE LEADERSHIP WHEEL

In the portal, you'll find the Leadership Wheel, which is the same tool I used with David.

Each spoke represents a vital area of leadership:

- Vision & Strategy
- Communication
- Emotional Intelligence
- Decision Making
- Adaptability
- Team Development
- Accountability
- Innovation

This isn't just a reflection tool. It's a mirror with a message. You'll rate yourself from one to ten in each area, not to critique, but to *reveal*. And then you'll ask yourself:

- Where am I leading with presence and clarity?

- Where am I defaulting to performance or disconnect?
- Where might my team be seeing a different version of me than I think I'm showing?

Bonus move: Be bold like David. Share the Wheel with your team. Ask for honest feedback. Let them rate you. Not as a verdict, but as a mirror. Not to tear you down, but to wake you up.

Because once you see it, you can shift it.

THOUGHT SHIFTER

Your Whole-Self Leadership Inventory

Ask yourself:

1. When do I lead from performance instead of presence?

_____

_____

_____

_____

_____

2. Where do I override my emotional signals instead of honoring them?

_____

_____

_____

_____

_____

_____

3. What am I modeling to my team when I skip self-care or overdeliver?

_____

_____

_____

_____

_____

4. How could I shift one part of my leadership to include more mind, emotion, energy, or soul? How might I nurture my whole self more?

_____

_____

_____

_____

_____

5. What ripple would that create, not just for my team, but for myself?

_____

_____

_____

_____

_____

You don't need a new system. You need a deeper source. Because when your leadership includes your whole self . . . your leadership becomes whole for everyone.

CHAPTER 9

· · · · · · · · · · ·

FEEDBACK IS A MIRROR, NOT A WEAPON

Feedback. Just reading the word might make your shoulders tense. For most people, feedback is loaded with anxiety, fear of judgment, memories of past criticism, or pressure to "fix" something. Why wouldn't it be like that? I remember hearing, "This is constructive criticism" . . . How in the *heck* do you criticize someone constructively?! Those two words do *not* belong in any sentence together if you're building relationships, teams, or trust. Feedback is expansion in motion. It's how we grow self awareness, deepen connection, strengthen trust, and stretch into better ways of being together. It opens the door for clarity, alignment, and real improvement. Solid feedback expands relationships, culture, and capacity. It shows people what's working, where there's a gap, and how to bridge it with intention. Feedback is not a weapon, a verdict, or a character assassination; it's a mirror. A calibration tool. A reflection of how your leadership is landing, not who you are at your core. When you shift your relationship with feedback, whether you're giving it or receiving it, everything expands: your communication, your presence, your influence, and your leadership impact. Feedback doesn't tear people down. When done right, it calls them up.

Let me introduce you to Rebecca. She was a creative force, expressive, high-energy, and full of heart. Her brain moved fast, and her ideas came faster. She lit up rooms. Clients loved her. But her boss, Joan? Not so much. Joan was numbers-driven, precise, and reserved. The kind of leader who thrives on logic, structure, and tight execution. She believed strong leadership meant staying professional, polished, and measured at all times. So when Rebecca received her first real piece of "constructive criticism" from Joan (yes, that is what Joan called it verbatim), it hit Rebecca hard. "Your energy is too much. You're too talkative in meetings. I need you to tone it down." That was it. No support. No context. No tools to shift or adapt, just a vague directive to *be less* of herself. When Rebecca asked what "toning it down" looked like, Joan responded, "You just need to be more professional."

Rebecca walked out of that meeting confused, discouraged, and honestly, a little angry. She wasn't trying to be unprofessional. She was passionate, engaged, and excited to lead and contribute. But her boss didn't know how to lead her because her style didn't fit Joan's mold. Joan didn't *get* Rebecca; therefore, she led her like a spreadsheet—cut out the "excess," tidy up the "output," and keep it linear. The problem? Rebecca was never meant to be linear. She was dynamic.

Eventually, Rebecca was let go. It crushed her. She cried. She questioned everything. And for a minute, she believed the problem *was* her. But here's where expansion did its thing. Rebecca quickly landed a new job under a leader who *saw her.* A leader who valued collaboration, encouraged creative input, and didn't need her to shrink her shine to feel secure. That leader gave feedback like this: "Rebecca, your energy brings life to the team. Let's channel it toward mentoring our newer hires; they could use a voice like yours."

That's feedback from a leader who gets it. A leader who sees strength and calls it forward, not in. A leader who knows how to expand what they want instead of shutting it down. Rebecca thrived. She was promoted twice within a year. And not because she changed who she was, but because someone finally reflected her strengths instead of trying to erase them.

The next time you're tempted to critique someone's style, pause. Ask: *Am I giving them a weapon or a mirror? Am I leading them, or just managing my own discomfort with their difference?* Feedback done right doesn't silence someone. It activates them.

One of the biggest myths in leadership is that **"feedback is the truth."** It's not. Feedback is a *truth* filtered through someone else's lens, emotions, and expectations. It doesn't define you. But it can inform you. That doesn't mean it's irrelevant. It means you have to receive it wisely. Strong leaders don't treat feedback as gospel. They treat it as data. Not every piece of feedback deserves your reaction. But every piece of feedback deserves your curiosity.

When feedback comes, ask yourself:

- Is this pointing to a blind spot I haven't seen?
- Is this about my tone, not just my words?
- Is there a kernel of truth here, even if it's wrapped messily?

When someone gives you feedback, they're telling you how your energy, behavior, or words impacted *them*. It's their perception.

HOW TO EXPAND FEEDBACK INTO GROWTH

If you want a feedback-rich environment, start modeling what it looks like to give and receive feedback without ego, defense, or shutdown. A feedback culture begins with you.

1. Be the Invitation

Feedback isn't something you demand. It's something you *invite*. How you normalize feedback depends on how you model it—how you ask for it, receive it, and stay open without collapsing, defending, or retaliating.

Expansion Modeling Phrases:

- "Thank you for that—I didn't realize I was coming off that way."
- "That's helpful. I need a moment to sit with it before I respond."
- "Is there something I could do differently next time?"

When you invite feedback, you normalize it. When you receive it with openness, you create safety. When you don't collapse under it or weaponize it in return, you build trust. Feedback isn't about calling people *out*. It's about calling people *forward*. And that starts with you.

If you want a feedback-rich culture, you must first create feedback-safe energy. You are the energy system in which your team and relationships live.

2. Build the Bridge Before You Cross It

You've heard it before: "People don't care what you know until they know that you care." Same goes for feedback. If your team or partner doesn't feel psychologically safe with you, if they don't believe you're rooting for them or that their growth matters to you, even well-intentioned feedback will feel like a threat. Feedback without a relationship feels like an attack. If people don't trust your intention, even well-meaning feedback can feel like a threat.

Build relational safety by expanding:

- Mutual respect
- Trust earned over time
- Clear communication about your true intentions

Don't throw feedback across a broken bridge. Build it first, with empathy, consistency, and presence. You can say hard things with grace. But if there's no relationship? It might just feel like criticism.

3. Coach, Don't Correct

Correction shrinks. Coaching expands. Correction says, "You messed up." Coaching says, "Let's figure it out together." When you coach someone, you're helping them think, grow, and take ownership. You're asking questions that pull out insight. When you correct someone, especially with edge or ego, you're creating hierarchy, pressure, and possibly shame. Leaders who correct from frustration usually get compliance. Leaders who coach from curiosity cultivate confidence and buy-in.

Expansion Coaching Questions:

- "Share with me what you think happened."
- "How would you approach it differently next time?"
- "What support do you need to succeed?"

You're not just managing tasks and outcomes. You're expanding humans.

4. Anchor Feedback in Ownership, Not Outcome

Feedback works when it creates movement, not just moments. When it's rooted in ownership, people shift from defensiveness into growth. It's not about blame, but it's about clarity, accountability, and forward motion.

Anchor it with questions that open doors, not that shut people down:

- "What's one shift you're ready to own moving forward?"
- "What's the real learning here?"
- "What strengths can we expand while making this adjustment?"

This isn't about calling someone out; it's about calling them forward into their next level.

5. Make Feedback a Two-Way Street

Strong leaders don't just give feedback. They model it, invite it, and grow from it. Real feedback cultures are built when people feel safe to speak up and know you're listening. It's not about evaluating everyone else from the sidelines. It's about asking, "What don't I see yet? And how can you help me lead better?" That's not weakness. That's whole-self leadership in action.

Power-FULL Feedback Questions:

- What can you tell me about my leadership that I might not see in myself?
- What's one thing that makes working with (or for) me harder than it needs to be?
- What's something you wish I understood better about your experience?
- If I could shift just one thing to be a stronger leader for you, what would it be?

The goal is partnership. You don't have to be perfect and act on every piece of feedback, but you do have to be willing to *listen*. When people feel heard, they lean in. And when you model openness, you don't just expand your leadership; you expand your trust, your impact, and your team's capacity to grow.

Feedback is a living, breathing conversation, not a top-down command. And when you lead that conversation with presence, humility, and expansion, you stop managing people and start activating them.

LAUREN AND THE "HARD TO WORK WITH" LABEL

Lauren was a director at a mid-sized marketing firm. Brilliant, bold, and razor-sharp. The kind of person who could walk into a room and solve problems that had everyone else spinning for five days in five minutes. Strategic to the bone. Passionate about results. But she'd been handed a label that stuck like glue: **"Hard to work with."** That was the feedback. Period. No conversation. No clarity. Just a casual comment from her manager: "People say you're hard to work with." And that was it. Lauren came into our coaching session fuming. "Are you kidding me? I deliver. I hit deadlines. I save their asses. And now I'm diffi-cult because I don't sugarcoat things?" I heard her. She wasn't wrong. But she wasn't landing either. So I asked her: "What if the problem isn't what you're saying, but how it's being felt?" That one cracked the door open.

We explored the difference between *intention* and *impact*. Lauren didn't mean to shut people down; she just wanted things done right and fast. But her intensity, clipped tone, and zero-room-for-error approach left a wake of tension. She wasn't being toxic; she was misaligned and uncalibrated. She thought she was modeling excellence, but to her team, she was modeling fear.

So we created a challenge: Ask five people for real feedback. Not a performance review. A human check-in. Here's what we came up with: "I want to be a better leader and teammate. Would you be open to shar-ing one way I've positively impacted you and one way I could grow?"

At first, she hated this exercise. "This feels soft," she said. "This feels like I'm asking them to coddle me." But she did it. And what came back cracked her wide open:

- "You're brilliant. But it feels like there's no room to make mis-takes around you."
- "You push us to be better, but sometimes it's like you forget we're human."
- "I admire your drive. But I don't always feel safe to speak up."

Those comments didn't break her. They woke her up because finally she could see what her leadership was expanding and what it was unintentionally crushing.

She didn't overhaul everything overnight. She made small shifts. She started pausing before responding and asking one more question before offering her opinion. She began acknowledging effort before redirecting. She practiced eye contact and breathing when she felt herself getting impatient. These weren't performative "nice girl" moves. These were strategic recalibrations of presence. And slowly, the energy shifted. People started coming to her more and asking for her input, trusting her intent. Her influence expanded not because she dialed herself down, but because she finally aligned how she showed up with who she wanted to be. **That's what whole-self leadership does.** It doesn't strip your edge. It sharpens your impact. And feedback? It stops feeling like an attack . . . and starts becoming your greatest expansion tool.

THOUGHT SHIFTER

Mirror Moments

Feedback is a powerful mirror. It's about being real, not "right."
Use this check-in:

1. What piece of feedback have I resisted? What might be underneath that resistance?

---

2. How do I usually respond to feedback: defense, collapse, or curiosity?

---

3. What kind of feedback culture am I modeling—at home, work, or in my community?

_____

_____

_____

_____

4. Who have I been avoiding giving feedback to? What truth needs to be shared?

_____

_____

_____

_____

5. Where might I be correcting instead of coaching?

_____

_____

_____

_____

Bonus Expansion

Do as Lauren did. Ask five people (or more): "I want to be a better leader and teammate. Would you be open to sharing one way I've impacted you positively . . . and one way I could grow?"

Feedback, when used with care and clarity, becomes one of your most powerful leadership tools.

So the next time it comes your way? Don't dodge the mirror. Stand in it. And expand.

CHAPTER 10

BOSS ENERGY VS. LEADERSHIP ENERGY

WHO'S REALLY IN THE ROOM?

Before a single directive leaves your mouth, your energy has already spoken. Leadership isn't just about direction; it's about transmission. Your tone, posture, and presence are either creating safety or shutting it down. They are either inspiring ownership or breeding silence. They are either expanding trust or reinforcing fear.

Because you're always leading, ask yourself, are you leading with boss energy or leadership energy? Boss energy shows up to manage outcomes. Leadership energy shows up to grow, develop, and expand people to their greatest level. Boss energy is about control, certainty, and authority. Leadership energy is about clarity, curiosity, and connection. Bosses direct. Leaders develop. Bosses issue orders. Leaders build capacity. Bosses micromanage. Leaders magnify.

You could be a frontline manager or a CEO. If your energy walks in the room and says, "I don't trust you," guess what? They won't trust themselves either. This is about transmission and how you make others *feel*.

BOSS ENERGY VS. LEADERSHIP ENERGY—
A QUICK HIT LIST

Boss Energy	Leadership Energy
Leads with authority.	Leads with alignment.
Drives results through pressure.	Inspires action through purpose.
Tells you what to do.	Helps you see what you're capable of.
Fears being questioned.	Welcomes dialogue and insight.
Expects compliance.	Cultivates ownership.
Creates dependency.	Builds capability.
Stays in control.	Shares power with clarity.
Commands, tells, and controls.	Inspires, mentors, and influences.
Demands respect.	Embodies respect.
Uses people to meet goals.	Invests in people to grow together.
Thinks short-term and reaction-based.	Operates with a long-term, vision-driven strategy.
Operates above the team.	Moves with the team.
Disciplines to correct.	Mentors to develop.

Marcus was the kind of operations director most companies dream about. Sharp, process-minded, always five steps ahead. He knew the numbers. He knew the business. And he thought he knew his team. But when he came into our coaching session, something was off. "I don't get it," he said. "I give clear instructions. I outline goals. I follow up. But the team? Disconnected. Sloppy. Like they're going through the motions." Deadlines were slipping. Engagement was low. He was frustrated. And under that frustration? He was confused. "I'm doing everything right," he insisted. "Why aren't they responding?" We pulled back. Slowed down. Looked at not just *what* he was saying, but *how* he was showing up. The words were fine. The strategy was sound. But the **energy**? That was the hidden problem.

Marcus was walking into every meeting with heat behind his eyes and weight in his shoulders. His tone was clipped. His presence was all urgency. His team didn't feel led; they felt managed. And not in a good way. I asked him one question: "What energy might your team tell us walks into the room before you do?"

Cue the pause. ". . .Probably a little intense," he admitted.

"Okay," I said. "Now be honest. Is that the kind of energy that invites solutions? Or shuts them down?"

That landed. We started small. I gave Marcus one simple recalibration practice: Five minutes before each meeting to *pause, breathe,* and *reset.*

No emails.

No notes.

No task review.

Just five minutes of stillness to ask:

What energy do I want to bring in?

How do I want them to feel when I speak?

What version of me will best serve this moment?

That's it. Simple. But it's not easy. At first, Marcus resisted. "I don't have time to breathe before meetings," he told me flatly.

"Then you don't have time to lead," I replied.

He left that session visibly irritated. I could feel the "this is ridiculous" energy trailing behind him like cologne that should've come with a hazard warning—loud, lingering, and completely unnecessary." And honestly? I wasn't sure what I'd get when we circled back two weeks later. He's a data guy. Systems thinker. Raised in a "don't cry; don't flinch; get it done" kind of home. He built his reputation on grit, not groundedness. So when I asked for his takeaways from our last session, I braced for sarcasm.

Instead, he leaned in and said, "Alright, I got over myself." (His words; not mine.) He told me he'd decided to play the "breath game" just to prove it wouldn't work. The first few attempts? Awkward as hell. Sitting still for five minutes felt like five hours. His brain raced with everything he *could* do: emails, prep, metrics, efficiency. But he kept at it. Day by day, something shifted. He started actually *noticing* his breath, where it was landing, how shallow it had become. How often he'd been operating in full-blown reaction mode, completely disconnected from his body. He realized he had been walking into meetings already wired, eyes darting, heart pounding, energy leaking pressure without saying a single word. Then came the science. He looked it up, because of course he did. And when he read that **intentional breathing activates the parasympathetic nervous system**, lowering cortisol, regulating emotional reactivity, and restoring focus? That's when it stopped feeling like fluff and started clicking as a function.

Marcus admitted something powerful: "Growing up, nobody in my house ever talked about breathing. Heck, breath work was never anything I heard or learned about. I didn't know it was even a thing. We pushed. We performed. We moved fast and kept it together. I didn't know slowing down could be a leadership skill." He wasn't just slowing his breath. He was retraining his nervous system and rewiring his brain all at the same time. With every inhale, he was reprogramming the part that had learned urgency equals value. Once that clicked, so did his presence. He started every meeting with three deep breaths, silently, for himself, not the team. He placed a sticky note on his laptop that said, "Take a breath and choose your energy." He even began tracking his "internal weather" in his notes—stormy, calm, windy, grounde —just to bring awareness to what his team might be walking into before he opened his mouth.

It was weird. It was new. And it worked. He chose to put his whole self in and lead. What changed? His beliefs about leadership. And

Boss Energy vs. Leadership Energy

when the beliefs shifted? So did everything else: his energy, his presence, his team's response. This was nervous system mastery and energy awareness. He started showing up grounded. Slower. More open. Same goals. Same strategy. But his tone softened. His shoulders dropped. His team noticed. Without a single memo, the room changed. One of his quietest team members pulled him aside after a meeting and said, "I don't know what you're doing differently . . . but I actually feel like you see us now."

Let me be clear: Marcus didn't change the *content* of his leadership. He changed the *energy* of it.

And that was everything. Because energy isn't fluff; it's a strategy that shapes safety. It fuels innovation. It opens conversations that your agenda alone never will. Marcus learned what so many leaders miss: Leadership isn't just about what you *say*. It's about what people *feel* when you say it. And if your energy walks into the room before your words do, why wouldn't you make damn sure it's the energy that leads well?

Let's be clear: Your energy is bigger than just influencing the room. Your energy becomes the room. It becomes how people respond, whether they speak up or shrink, and whether your culture is expanding or surviving.

So here is where you pause and ask:

- What am I expanding with my presence?
- What do people feel when I enter the room?
- What am I modeling that's being mirrored back?

Energy is the silent communicator. It conveys confidence, empathy, urgency, or calmness without uttering a single word. Your team picks up on this energy, consciously or not, and responds accordingly. When your energy aligns with your words, trust is built. When it doesn't, dissonance arises. To lead effectively, here are three things to cultivate awareness of your energy:

127

1. **Self reflection**: Regularly assess your emotional and mental state.
2. **Mindfulness practices**: Engage in activities that center you, like meditation, breathwork with deep breathing, EFT (tapping), or journaling, to name a few that we recommend.
3. **Feedback loops**: Seek input on how others perceive your presence.

You can adjust and align your energy with your leadership goals by tuning in to your energy. Your energy can inspire action, foster collaboration, and drive innovation. It can also hinder progress if misaligned.

THOUGHT SHIFTER

Energy Audit

Grab that pen and reflect on the following:

1. What energy do I consistently project in my leadership role or bring into my meetings, conversations, and decisions?

_____

_____

_____

_____

2. How does my energy affect or influence my team's morale, performance, and outcomes?

_____

_____

_____

_____

3. What practices can I adopt to enhance my energetic presence and support my leadership objectives?

_____

_____

_____

_____

Bonus Practice: Energy Check

Take three to five minutes before your next meeting or conversation. Take three deep breaths and ask yourself:

1. What energy am I currently radiating?

_____

_____

_____

_____

2. Is it aligned with what I want this moment to feel like?

_____

_____

_____

_____

3. What might others be picking up from me, even if I'm silent?

_____

_____

_____

4. What's one shift I can make (in breath, posture, tone, intention) to lead more clearly?

_____

_____

_____

_____

5. How do I want them to *feel* when they walk away?

_____

_____

_____

_____

Energy leads. Words follow. Lead with alignment. Lead with presence. Lead with intention.

CHAPTER 11

BURNOUT

IS WHAT YOU ARE HOLDING,
NOT JUST DOING

Let's call burnout what it really is. It's not just a full calendar. It's the full emotional backpack you've been dragging from meeting to meeting. It's what you've been *holding*, not just doing. Burnout isn't simply about having too much to *do*. It's about having too much to *hold*. Too many unspoken expectations. Too much emotional labor. Too many identity hats. There were too many roles, all worn at once, and there was nowhere to set them down. And in leadership? That load gets heavier.

You're not just leading tasks. You're absorbing trauma, tension, and everyone else's timelines while pretending you're fine. That's not leadership; that's martyrdom in a blazer. It comes with the responsibility of being the one people turn to. The one who has to "keep it together." The one who absorbs everyone else's urgency, anxiety, needs, and projections. You're not just managing outcomes.

You're managing:

- Team morale
- Client tension
- Family expectations

- Inner pressure to prove you're enough

And the most dangerous part? That invisible weight? Most leaders carry it. They've normalized it. They don't even realize it's there until they finally set it down.

BURNOUT IS WHAT HAPPENS WHEN YOU ABANDON YOURSELF WHILE LEADING OTHERS

Let that sink in.

Most leaders don't burn out because they don't care. They burn out because they *care too much*, for too long, without replenishment. Without boundaries. Without a safe place to put down the mask and exhale. Let's redefine what it means to be "burnt out." It's not just exhaustion. It's emotional depletion. Energetic collapse. It's when your leadership becomes a performance instead of a presence.

THE "STRONG ONE" SYNDROME

If you're the one who "holds it all," this one's for you.

You know how to carry the meeting, the team, the emotions, and the space. You know how to smile and say, "I've got it," even when your soul whispers, "I don't know how much longer I can hold this."

Sound familiar?

It's not weakness. It's the *accumulation* of self abandonment. The internal agreement is that everyone else's needs come before your own. But take this in: *You can't lead what you refuse to nourish.* And that includes you.

You don't teach your team how to thrive by burning yourself down to keep the lights on. That's not expansion. That's erosion. We can't forget why we are here, so I must ask: What are you expanding in your leadership when you do not take care of yourself? What are you telling everyone around you? What message are they getting about leadership? Leaders are to inspire other leaders; what will they want to follow in you when you choose not to take care of yourself?

RICK AND THE SLOW BURN

Rick looked successful on the outside: back-to-back meetings, inbox at zero, always available. But under the surface, he was unraveling. His calendar said "leadership." His body said "collapse." Rick was the kind of leader every mission-driven organization dreams of: heart on fire, sleeves rolled up, always on. As the director of a growing nonprofit, he lived and breathed the mission. His team admired him. His board praised him. He was the kind of leader people write articles about. But behind the passion was a quiet storm. Rick was running on fumes. He skipped meals. He fired off 2 a.m. emails and told his team to "take care of yourselves" while skipping his vacations and replying to messages during family dinners. He was always in go mode. Always carrying the weight. And it was catching up to him.

In one of our coaching sessions, he exhaled and said, "I feel like I'm fading. Like I'm here . . . but I'm not." That sentence stopped us both. We didn't start with productivity hacks or a new calendar. Rick didn't need a better planner. He needed a better pattern. We did an energy inventory. Not a breakdown of his meetings, but a breakdown of where his energy was actually going. What was draining it? Where was it leaking? And what was weighing on him that wasn't even on his to-do list. It hit fast. Rick was holding space for a grieving employee, managing a looming funding gap, trying to calm a board with shifting expectations, supporting his partner through their burnout, and carrying this deep fear that if *he* slowed down, everything would fall apart. He was leading from the place so many leaders do: over-functioning with good intentions and no capacity. He wasn't broken. He was exhausted. And what he needed wasn't a performance tweak, it was permission to be human. So we rebuilt his rhythm from the inside out.

Rick began scheduling recovery time as if it were a board meeting—non-work mornings, walks, playlists that recharged him, golf with friends, and yes, meditation and breathwork. Not nice-to-haves, but *non-negotiables*. He trained his leadership team in co-regulation and emotional agility so he wasn't the only one holding the energy of the room. He set new response boundaries: no emails past 7 p.m., full presence at the dinner table, complete disconnection on weekends. And maybe most importantly? He created a reflection space. A thirty-minute weekly check-in, not just to look at what he accomplished, but to ask himself: *How did I feel doing it? What's working? What's not?* The ripple for Rick was instant. Some people take a little longer, but Rick was ready. He knew that if something didn't change, the cost of staying the same would actually cost him more than the change itself. His commitment and courage to make the change paid off. His team felt it. Productivity increased. Meetings got shorter. Engagement went up, not down. One of his employees said, "You feel more grounded. It makes me feel aligned and excited to be here."

Even his donors noticed. Two months in, a longtime funding partner increased their donation, saying, "Something feels different around here, like there's a deeper focus and passion to the mission again." Because Rick had stopped being the energetic martyr and started becoming the energetic model. He didn't need to quit his job. He just needed to quit abandoning himself. That's when he began leading again, not from fumes, but from fullness.

YOUR NERVOUS SYSTEM IS YOUR LEADERSHIP FOUNDATION

You can't fake grounded energy. If your nervous system is fried, your leadership is shaky.

You'll react instead of respond. You'll snap instead of support. You'll perform instead of connect.

Burnout isn't a badge of honor. It's a signal. It's your body whispering, "I need you, too."

SIGNS YOU'RE HOLDING TOO MUCH

- You feel emotionally numb or overly reactive

- Rest feels guilt-inducing instead of restorative
- You crave isolation more than connection
- Your inner dialogue sounds like "just get through the day"
- Even small tasks feel insurmountable

If this is you, pause. Ask yourself: *What am I holding that was never mine to carry alone?*

THOUGHT SHIFTER

The Burnout Reboot

Take five to ten quiet minutes. Reflect honestly:

1. What emotional weights am I carrying that no one sees?

_____

_____

_____

2. What am I over-functioning for — and why?

_____

_____

_____

3. What boundaries have I abandoned to "keep the peace" or "be the strong one"?

_____

_____

_____

_____

4. What does my body need right now that I've been ignoring?

_____

_____

_____

_____

5. What would shift if I believed my well-being were non-negotiable?

_____

_____

_____

_____

Self-abandonment in leadership isn't sustainable. It's a countdown to collapse. But when you lead from wholeness—when your nervous system is calm, your boundaries are clear, and your energy is rooted? You don't just survive. You expand this greatness. And everyone around you rises with you.

. . . .

CHAPTER 12

HOLDING IT ALL IS
HOLDING YOU BACK

There's a story too many leaders are still stuck inside: "If I can just hold it all, keep it moving, and stay in control . . . we'll be okay." Control can feel like leadership when your nervous system is on high alert, when past failures are still fresh. When you've built success by muscling through and you're scared to loosen the grip. But holding it all is holding you back.

Control builds distance, not trust. Distance from your team, from your purpose, from yourself.

Your team is a team of leaders entrusted to you, and what most of them crave the most is clarity, not control. Clarity on roles, expectations, values, boundaries, and what actually matters. When clarity is missing, control fills the gap. It becomes the default move. Micromanaging. Over-functioning. Avoiding delegation. Overworking. Not because you're a control freak, but because your nervous system is trying to keep you safe.

Control is the armor leaders wear when they're carrying too much and can't afford to drop the ball. But the problem with armor? You can't connect through it. Many leaders aren't power-hungry; they're survival-smart. They've been burned. Blindsided. Betrayed.

They're carrying business PTSD—what my coach, Sara Connell, calls B-PTSD. It doesn't show up as flashbacks. It shows up as procrastination, overwhelm, imposter syndrome, avoidance, always being "on" but never really present. It whispers things like: "If I stop holding everything, it will fall apart," "If I let go, someone will screw it up and it'll be on me," and "If I admit I'm tired, they'll think I can't lead." These are patterns, self-protection dressed as productivity. If your old wounds are running your leadership, you're not leading, you're surviving. Expansion requires something braver: the willingness to trust that you don't have to do it all to lead powerfully.

You just have to lead what's yours, clearly, courageously, and in alignment.

DANIEL'S GRIP ON EVERYTHING

Daniel was the founder of a high-growth tech startup. Visionary. Driven. Sharp as hell.

But trusting? Not even close. He reviewed every client call. Held every decision. Micromanaged every metric. Why? Because one bad hire early on had tanked a major project. It left a scar, which has been running the show ever since. When we started coaching, he came in hot:

"My team's not stepping up. They can't handle what's at stake. If I don't keep control, I'll lose everything."

So I asked him, "What does 'everything' mean to you?"

He paused. "My credibility. My team. What we've built. My name. My place in this space."

I asked again, "Where did you learn that if you let go, it would all fall apart?" That's when he exhaled. One of those deep, soul-clearing sighs. "Growing up . . . if you didn't stay in control, someone else took everything. Took your credit. Took your power. Took your shot."

And there it was.

Daniel wasn't leading from vision. He was leading from defense. The grip was about survival, not strategy.

His first shift? Weekly energy awareness check-ins. Before every leadership meeting, Daniel took 3–5 minutes to breathe, ground, and name the energy he wanted to bring. That alone changed the tone in the room. People started showing up differently. Less guarded. More engaged. He started an energy journal where he documented when his energy was off and when he was judging and not listening. That made him aware of how much it was showing up. Even in his everyday personal things, he kept the exercise going.

Next? He started delegating, not just tasks, but decisions. I helped him identify one trusted leader and gave him a challenge: "This week, let them lead a meeting without your input. No edits. No 'just in case' backups. Let it be theirs." It rattled him a bit. But he did it. And they crushed it.

So we built more from there. Daniel built a "Trust Map," an actual doc breaking down:

- What he still controlled
- What could be co-led
- What needed to be handed off entirely

He had to name what was based on fear versus what actually required his oversight. We also did a reset meeting with the team and trained them on how to *receive* that trust and create conversation around it when they felt Daniel was reverting to fear. As Daniel grew, the team grew. They didn't just get more responsibility, they got more clarity. We created a weekly "What I'm Letting Go" ritual. One thing. Every week. One thing he used to hold too tightly that he consciously released or shared. And then we started working on his nervous system:

- Box breathing before big meetings
- Reframing fear-based thoughts in real-time
- Practicing co-regulation with his team
- Journaling to track emotional triggers

He started to sleep again. His body softened. His thinking expanded. For the first time in years, Daniel went on a vacation and didn't check his phone once. His team didn't fall apart. They rose.

When Daniel learned to trust his team and himself, everything changed.

Want your people to rise? Trust them.

Want to scale your impact? Loosen the grip.

Want to lead without burnout? Co-regulate. Don't control.

Ask yourself:

- What am I trying to protect by staying in control?
- What am I afraid will happen if I let go?
- What am I teaching my team by how I show up?

Trust opens and expands your team. This leadership shares the weight. A fortress is no longer needed on this foundation.

THOUGHT SHIFTER

The Control Detox

1. What area of my leadership feels the tightest right now?

_____

_____

_____

_____

2. What story is keeping me stuck in that pattern?

_____

_____

_____

_____

3. What fear am I believing that's asking for clarity instead of control?

_____

_____

_____

_____

4. Where can I safely hand off ownership this week?

_____

_____

_____

_____

5. What's one micro shift that would show my team what trust looks like?

_____

_____

_____

_____

You don't have to hold it all. Lead what's yours with clarity, courage, and presence.

CHAPTER 13

360 LEADERSHIP

LEADING UP, ACROSS, WITHIN, AND AROUND

Y ou're here to influence, model, challenge, and expand in every direction—with your team, peers, boss, clients, and yourself. Leadership doesn't move in one direction. You're not here just to manage people who report to you. How do I know that? You're reading this book, aren't you? *Wink wink.* You're here to make a difference, not just in your role but every room you walk into. And to do that, you've got to make sure nothing in you is quietly blocking that impact or clogging your clarity.

Welcome to **360 Leadership,** where you lead up, across, within, and around.

Let's break it down:

- **Leading up** means you speak truth with courage and clarity to those in positions of authority. You don't shrink, perform, or manipulate. You lead with grounded influence.

- **Leading across** means you collaborate without competing. You meet your peers in alignment, not ego. You show up real, not rehearsed.
- **Leading within** means you take the inner work seriously. If you don't lead yourself, your mindset, emotions, and energy, you'll lead from your wounds. And everyone will feel it.
- **Leading around** is the energetic residue you leave behind in your conversations, meetings, and messages. It's not just about your words; it's about your wake in every area of your life, both personal and professional.

This is whole-self leadership in motion. Your beliefs, emotions, choices, and presence are all pulling in the same direction. That's how trust builds, cultures shift, and impact sticks.

How do you walk into the room? How do you leave people feeling once you've walked out?

What energy are you expanding, whether someone's watching or not? Leadership is a verb.

It's action. It's alignment. It's energy. And how you live it . . . is exactly what you lead.

360 LEADERSHIP: FROM THEORY TO PRACTICE

1. Leading Up

Most people shrink when it comes to managing up. They either play it safe, kiss ass, or go silent when something feels off.

But here's your cue:

If you're afraid to speak truth to power, you're still performing, not leading.

Leading up means you:

- Communicate proactively, not just reactively
- Respectfully challenge decisions when needed

- Make your leader's life easier *and* more honest

You don't lead up with ego; you lead up with clarity. You don't lead up to impress; you lead up to align. And yes, it takes guts. But if your truth is always waiting until it's "safe," you're not really leading, you're surviving.

QUICK STORY:

Maria was a regional operations lead who sat in silence during executive meetings until the day she spoke up about a policy she knew was tanking morale on the ground. She wasn't angry or defensive, just clear. Her voice shook, but her message landed. That meeting changed her credibility. She went from "compliant" to "trusted."

2. Leading Across

This one gets messy. Peers. Coworkers. Fellow leaders. The people who are "on your level" but—let's be honest—sometimes feel like competition, comparison triggers, or emotional landmines.

Leading across means:

- Dropping the ego and collaborating like grown-ass humans
- Naming the tension instead of avoiding it
- Celebrating each other's wins without shrinking or puffing up

Want to know your leadership maturity? Look at how you handle your peers' success. If you're secretly threatened by it, good news: that's your growth edge. Powerful leaders don't shrink for crumbs. They rise and invite others to the table.

QUICK STORY

After losing a big client to her peer's team, Lillie almost spiraled into resentment. Instead, she texted a genuine congrats, then asked to grab coffee and learn what had worked. That one coffee turned into a collaboration that doubled their division's numbers in the fourth quarter. She rose by rising together.

3. Leading Within

Let's not forget the root of them all.

While leading others can be impressive, leading *yourself* is what determines them all.

- Do you self-regulate when you're triggered?
- Do you tell yourself the truth even when it's uncomfortable?
- Do you course-correct without spiraling in shame?

This isn't about toxic positivity or pretending you're fine. This is about your mindset beliefs, emotional leadership, and energy vibrational output. About choosing your tone, presence, and responses on purpose and with intention. You want to lead with power? It starts within, with truth.

QUICK STORY

Kyle was known for his emotional blowups until one coaching session hit different. He realized his outbursts were about control, not clarity. The next time tension flared, he paused, took a breath, and simply asked, "What are you needing from me right now, and what will this decision expand?" That one shift changed his influence overnight.

4. Leading Around

This is where leadership meets life. Not the role. Not the title. The *you* underneath it all.

All-around leadership isn't about what you do in your job. It's about how you move through the world. It's who you are when it's hard. When no one's watching. When you're not "on."

It's how you show up—in the workplace *and* in your kitchen. The team meeting *and* the text thread. It's how you treat the slow barista, the crying toddler, the overwhelmed friend, and the mistake you made.

Around means everywhere, every moment, in all directions. You're being in all things. It's the love you lead with at home. The boundaries you hold with grace. The presence you bring to your people. The energy you pour into your purpose.

Leading around, in all directions, is whole-self expansion. Because how you lead one space, you eventually lead *all* spaces.

MARCO, THE MID-LEVEL MANAGER WHO LED EVERYWHERE

Marco didn't have the title yet. Mid-level manager. No direct reports. No corner office. No formal power. But presence? That he had eventually, but not at first.

I'll never forget Marco's first day in a leadership group coaching series we were doing for his company. Twenty-nine other frontline leaders were in the virtual room, all new to leadership, all there to expand. Marco came in quiet . . . but not in a grounded kind of way. The kind of quiet that hides behind sarcasm. He cracked jokes. Distracted others. Nervous energy masked as humor. And when he showed up late? There was always a reason. Tech issues. Client calls. Too busy. By the third session, I reached out privately. Not to reprimand, but to reflect. "Marco," I said, "how you show up *here* is how you show up *there*. This space is leadership. So what are you modeling? What are you teaching the room about your leadership through how you're arriving, engaging, and contributing?"

That moment landed. I saw it in his face, the "oh, damn" realization. It wasn't about being wrong. It was about being *seen*.

From that day forward, he stopped performing . . . and started leading. He showed up early, not just to be on time, but to set the tone. He didn't hog airtime; he asked powerful, curious questions that moved the entire conversation forward. He offered insights without dominance. He listened like he meant it. And by the end of the twelve-week experience? Marco had become the informal leader of the room.

His peers respected him. They looked to him. They followed his lead, not because of a title, but because of his *alignment.*

Even his leaders noticed. The same Marco who started off cracking jokes to avoid vulnerability had become the one coaching up the chain, modeling emotional intelligence, and speaking with calm confidence during chaos.

He didn't wait to be a leader. He became one. One choice at a time. One question at a time. One shift at a time. One action, one accountability, one follow up at a time. Marco didn't rise because he chased a role. He rose because he owned his presence. And that? That's what leadership looks like, in every direction.

Your leadership is never limited to a title. It's expanded through how you show up everywhere. At your kid's school. On your team's Slack thread. In the hallway with a coworker. In the quiet moments when no one's watching. That's where real leadership lives. Your *frequency*, the energy you emit before you ever say a word, sets the tone. It matters because it's the vibe people feel when you walk into a room, the undercurrent of every interaction. It's not about volume or visibility; it's about *vibe.*

Your frequency doesn't wait for permission. It doesn't wait for the right role, the fancy title, or the spotlight. It's speaking now, with or without your awareness. And whether you're leading up, across, within, or all around, your frequency is either inviting trust . . . or repelling it. Creating safety . . . or leaking stress. Aligning energy . . . or amplifying misalignment. So, if you're wondering how to expand your influence? Don't look at your title. Look at your *tune.*

THOUGHT SHIFTER

360 Frequency Audit

Ready to check your current 360 frequency?

1. Where in my life am I waiting for a title, role, or "right moment" to lead?

_____

_____

_____

_____

2. How do I respond when a peer outshines me?

_____

_____

_____

_____

3. Where am I withholding truth from a leader I report to? Why?

_____

_____

_____

_____

_____

4. What's one way I can lead more powerfully *within* myself this week?

_____

_____

_____

_____

_____

5. What vibration do I want to leave in the rooms I walk into, regardless of hierarchy?

_____

_____

_____

_____

_____

You don't need a promotion to lead. You just need presence. Don't wait for permission to be powerful. Be powerful and lead from where you are.

· · · · · · · · · ·

CHAPTER 14

WHEN YOU LEAD LIKE YOU—NOT LIKE THEM

Trying to lead like someone else will strip your power faster than any failure ever will.

Let me tell you how I know. Back when I was stepping into this work, I didn't have a roadmap. Confidence? Wobbly. Voice? Filtered. Direction? All over the damn place. So, like many well-meaning over-achievers, I started piecing together a version of "leadership" based on what looked successful. If I needed to seem calm, I mimicked the poised one. If I needed to look bold, I channeled the edgy one. If I needed to be "professional," I toned everything down. I was patch-working personas, taking a little from here and a little from there. And on the outside? It worked. I looked the part. I knew the buzzwords. People bought in. But inside? I was drifting further and further from myself. Because none of those versions were actually me. I was in a web of growing ego and fear. Each move I made was based on percep-tion management, not aligned presence. And while I was technically "rising," I was also *shrinking*. My power wasn't rooted. My leadership wasn't honest. I wasn't expanding my abundance. I was mimicking and expanding confusion, duality, and loss. That's what happens when you're chasing fragments of everyone else's success instead of expanding from your own truth.

I remember the exact moment it caught up with me. I was invited to speak at a high-level leadership roundtable, a room full of decision-makers and C-suite executives whom I admired. It should have felt like a "hell yes" moment. But instead, I stood backstage staring at my notes and felt like a stranger to my own message. Suddenly, I didn't know which version of myself was supposed to walk out there. Was I the polished pro with the PowerPoint and perfect posture? Was I the wise, eloquent coach who drops the perfect question at the perfect time and doesn't flinch? Was I the calm, centered one who speaks in metaphors and mindfulness? I had studied all the styles. Borrowed all the tones. Built a toolkit of "how to show up," but not once did I stop to ask: *What does it mean to show up as ME?* And when they called my name, I froze. Not outwardly—I smiled, I stepped out, I delivered. But inside? I felt like an imposter, a stranger, a hollow version of myself. Present . . . but not *aligned*. Experiencing that feeling of "fake" and "you're not real" is the moment I knew I didn't just want a seat at the table, I wanted to *belong* at the table, and that only happens when the version of you sitting down . . . is the real one.

So what did I do next?

I got honest. Like, rip-off-the-Band-Aid, burn-the-fake-script, *look-in-the-mirror* honest. I admitted to myself and to the person who would become one of the most important mentors in my life that I didn't want to perform anymore. I wanted to *lead*, not just train, coach, or deliver solid content, but lead from a place so aligned that I could change rooms, conversations, and companies. And you know what she said? "Good. Then stop bullshitting yourself." She didn't coddle me. She didn't let me mimic. She didn't pat me on the head and tell me to find my voice someday. She *called it out* of me. Every call, every assignment, every challenge was a mirror and a microphone. She held me accountable to becoming the woman I said I wanted to be, not the one I thought I had to be to stay booked, liked, or "brand-appropriate."

We tore apart the scripts. We dismantled the templates. We realigned every part of my business and my energy around truth. I started writing content that sounded like *me*, not an industry standard. I stopped saying yes to clients who wanted polish without depth. I redesigned offers, rewrote my bios, and restructured my calendar. And I finally allowed my leadership to come from who I *am*, not who I thought I should be. Did it feel uncomfortable at first? Hell yes. But did it feel like *freedom*? You better believe it. Because here's the secret sauce no one tells you: When you show up as *you*, fully, freely, and unapologetically, your people don't just find you. They *feel* you. And when they feel you, they trust you. That's the kind of leadership that doesn't burn out. That's the kind of leadership that doesn't need a script. That's the kind of leadership that actually creates impact, not just image.

The moment you start comparing your leadership to someone else's, you cut off access to your own calibration. You tune out your instincts, override your intuition, and mimic their moves instead of listening to your own rhythm. You're expanding into a shape shifter, and before you know it, you're saying the right things with the wrong energy, nodding when you want to challenge, agreeing when inside, you're screaming, *this doesn't fit me!*

Meet my client, Marissa. Like most of my leaders, Marissa was the get-it-done kind of leader. Smart, high-functioning, and deeply respected. But beneath the surface, she was drowning.

Not because she didn't have the skills but because she was constantly contorting herself to fit a leadership style that looked good on paper but felt like performance art in real life.

And that's where our work began . . .

Marissa had just been promoted to supply chain manager. She was sharp, people-savvy, and brilliant at finding creative solutions that pulled her team together. The kind of ambivert who could dive into the details, keep everyone aligned, and still bring warmth to the process.

But when she stepped into her new role, something shifted—and not in the right direction.

Instead of leading like herself, she tried to lead like her vice president: bold, loud, and commanding the room. He was the kind of guy who took up space and made decisions quickly, and she thought, *well . . . that must be what leadership looks like.* She started lowering her voice, cutting people off in meetings, sharpening her tone, trying to "own the room" the way he did.

But it didn't land. Her team grew quiet. Collaboration dropped. Feedback started rolling in; she was "hard to read," "intense," even "tense to be around."

In a coaching session, I asked her, "What version of you do you feel most powerful in, not most impressive, but most grounded?" She froze. I waited and held the silence. She wanted me to fill the space with another question. I didn't.

Finally, she spoke: "The version of me that asks good questions. That listens. That sees patterns. That makes people feel like they matter."

Awareness at its finest. She could now go to work not just on her leadership skills, but on her mindset, emotions, beliefs, energy, and story, the way she wanted to write it.

She shared her past. How she was the quiet one in class who always knew the answer but was never called on fast enough. One of five siblings, squeezed into the chaos of sports, dance, and church activities, where the loudest voice got the spotlight. That "pick me" energy ran deep.

And the vice president? He was always picked, so it made sense that mimicking him felt like the way to "win" at leadership. But Marissa didn't need to become him; she needed to remember herself. We rebuilt her inner framework, rewiring her beliefs, recentering her voice, and realigning her leadership with who she *really* was. Her confidence took off; her energy shifted; and her leadership style became magnetic.

She learned how to lead one-on-one meetings with curiosity instead of control. She shared her processes instead of pretending to "just know." And she became an expert at delivering valuable feedback with empathy rather than an edge, causing her team not just to respond, but to rise, soar, and achieve the highest productivity levels in company history. People began seeking her out, not because she had a title but because she had *presence*.

Marissa didn't lead louder. She led from her truth. She stopped trying to lead like him. And started feeling and leading like herself.

YOU'RE THE MODEL, NOT THE MOLD

You weren't put here to fit the mold. You were put here to break the damn thing and build your own. When you lead from wholeness, not performance, you give other people permission to do the same.

So ask yourself:

- What part of my leadership have I been muting or editing to "fit in"?
- Where am I shrinking my presence to match someone else's comfort?
- What would it look like to lead with my whole self, even if it's different from the norm?

THOUGHT SHIFTER

Lead Like You

Grab your journal or a voice memo; let this one land in your bones.

1. Where have I been mimicking someone else's leadership style? Why?

---

2. What parts of my natural leadership have I been minimizing or hiding?

_____

_____

_____

3. When do I feel most like *myself* in a leadership moment?

_____

_____

_____

4. What would shift if I trusted that *my way* is *the way* for me?

_____

_____

_____

5. What's one bold or quiet move I could make this week that reflects who I *actually* am?

_____

_____

_____

You don't need to become someone else to lead well. You just need to come back home to yourself.

Own your tone. Own your truth. Own your energy, Lead like you.

CHAPTER 15

THE REAL POWER MOVE: ACCOUNTABILITY

I t's time to talk about the one thing every leader wants more of and the one thing that, when missing, will quietly (or loudly) unravel your entire team.

This is the make-or-break factor.

The pattern-shaper.

The mirror.

The muscle.

This is: accountability.

If leadership is your vehicle, then accountability? That's the engine.

You might resist it. You might avoid it. But without it, you're just spinning your wheels.

For a lot of people, even the word sends a chill down their spine. It brings flashbacks of micromanaging bosses, dreaded performance reviews, guilt trips, or getting thrown under the bus when things went sideways.

But let's flip that script. What if accountability weren't about blame but about ownership?

Not about control but about clarity? Not about pressure but about alignment? Because true accountability doesn't shrink people. It empowers them. And if you're serious about being the kind of leader people trust, follow, and rise with? This is where the real work begins.

To show you what that transformation looks like, let me introduce you to someone who lived it, mess and all . . .

MEET STEVEN: FROM BURNOUT TO BREAKTHROUGH

"Nobody understands the commitment I've given this company. I work nonstop. I've got so much unused PTO that I could take a sabbatical and still leave hours on the table. Lunch? Ha! That's a mythical concept. And now, after twenty damn years in leadership, they're telling me I need coaching? Coaching for emotional awareness and leadership competencies? Are you kidding me? That's bullshit!"

Yep. That was the energy I walked into.

Steven wasn't whispering, either. Through the thin office walls, I could hear every syllable of his rant loud and clear, but even louder than his words was the roar of his misunderstood heart. Tired. Resentful. Worn down. And if I'm being real, pissed. And rightfully so, from *his* perspective.

Year after year, Steven had been the one who stepped up. Fewer people. Higher targets. More pressure. Less time. And still, he delivered. Every damn time. Until, of course, there was nothing left of him to give.

When we started working together, he told me he had turned his car into a mobile office. Not metaphorically. *Literally.* A hotspot, a laptop, a dual monitor setup strapped into the passenger seat. He'd pull up to the baseball field where his kids played and "watch the game" while hammering out reports, answering Slack messages, and reviewing sales data from the West Coast.

Burnout? Honey, burnout left the building five years ago. This was a full-blown identity collapse masked as dedication.

He was down four employees and another manager, and instead of training anyone, Steven just kept doing it all himself. "It's faster if I just handle it myself," he'd say. "No one else will get it right anyway."

He loved the chaos. He thrived in it. But like any addiction, it turned on him. He couldn't feel joy anymore. Couldn't connect. Couldn't stop spinning long enough to notice he was running on fumes.

And it showed.

His team, once loyal, energized, and high-performing, was now rotating faster than a revolving door. Complaints stacked up. Human resources got involved. One employee used the word "abusive." Another said he was "exhausting to work for." And honestly, depending on which pair of glasses you were wearing, both might've been right. Because when you're operating from a deep pit of resentment, scarcity, and stress, you *will* leak that energy on your team, on your family, and on yourself.

That's where I came in.

I agreed to coach Steven—not because he was easy and not because he asked, but because I could see the fight *behind* the frustration. He still wanted to lead, but he didn't know how to lead from *expansion* instead of contraction.

Our first session? A complete two-and-a-half-hour soul purge. He vented. He defended. He baited me with victim mode (Level 1) and threw in some defiant finger pointing (Level 2) just for flair. And I let him.

Then I asked one question: "Steven, what do you want that you don't currently have?"

He dodged it at first. "They don't listen." "They don't care." "They're lazy."

So, I asked again.

And again.

Until finally, he exhaled. Big. Like all the way down to his gut. And then, the truth spilled out:

"I don't know what will make it better . . . I just want to love my job again. I want to be excited to come in. I want to do it damn good and feel damn good doing it."

And there it was. That was the moment I knew we were in. That this wasn't a lost cause. This was a *leader* who needed to find his own *light* again.

Fast forward two years: Steven is still with the company. But now? He leads with balance. He trains and trusts his team. He *unplugs*. He expanded out of chaos into ownership, growth, and accountability.

I'm telling you this story because it's how many of my clients show up. Worn down, used up, and ready to throw in the towel—but also ready to reclaim something deeper.

This isn't just leadership work. It's energy work. It's identity work. It's about choosing how you want to show up and what the heck you want to expand. Master that skill, and you'll become the kind of leader people actually want to follow. Not because you bark orders, but because you lead with clarity, consistency, and integrity. That, my friend, is the power of personal accountability. Don't overthink it, but what's the very first thought or reaction you have when you see the word.

ACCOUNTABILITY?

Love it? Hate it? Think it means blame? Control? Pressure? Honor? Ownership?

Grab a pen, take a moment, and write your gut-level answers down to the following:

1. Accountability is . . .
2. Accountability feels . . .
3. Accountable people are . . .
4. I am accountable when . . .

Don't explain, don't justify. Just answer. Getting to this layer of thought? That's where the shift starts, not in the perfect answer but in the honest one. Because this is the stuff that's actually running the show, and now you've brought it to the surface. Your subconscious beliefs about accountability are shaping how you lead right now. Whether you resist, avoid, or embrace it with arms wide open, it's creating your results. It's influencing how you handle mistakes, engage your team, and show up when things get messy (and they always do).

Back to Steven.

This man had a deeply tangled relationship with accountability. He confused it with blame. Every time the word came up in our coaching sessions, he flinched like I'd thrown a punch. His story of accountability was rooted in punishment. Every mistake? A threat. Every correction? A condemnation. No wonder he pushed back. But here's the shift that cracked his leadership wide open: Steven finally understood the power of accountability—and his lack thereof.

Accountability is not about fault. It's about ownership.

Steven realized he'd been giving his power away every time he blamed his team, human resources, the executives, or even the customers. Every time he deflected, he delayed his growth. And every time he took things personally? He stayed stuck in the very pain he wanted to escape.

That's when we flipped the switch. We made accountability his power tool.

Instead of asking, "Why is this happening to me?" he started asking, "What's my role in this, and how do I want to respond?" That shift was the beginning that changed everything.

Steven came into our next video session dragging. Not physically. He was still doing the superman, coffee in hand, "I got this" dance with a smile, but his energy was . . . cracked. Like his armor had finally thinned just enough for the light to start poking through.

This time, he was venting about another team member who had "an attitude," didn't "pull their weight," and "wasn't committed." He said, "I swear, these people just don't care like I do. They don't have pride in the work anymore."

And I said, "Steven, who taught them how to care?"

Silence.

Then he laughed. One of those dry, slightly-pained, "damn, that hit hard" kind of laughs. Because he knew he had unintentionally taught them that work equaled frenzy, effort equaled exhaustion, and leadership equaled martyrdom. And the truth is? He cared so much he'd forgotten how to show it without control and chaos.

"Steven," I asked gently but directly, "How might they be simply modeling the energy you've been leading with?"

He looked at me, held a stare right at me, and for the first time since I'd met him, he was not defensive. Not reactive. He was just quiet. He leaned back, looked at the whiteboard behind his desk, then at his laptop, then back at me. "Shit," he said. "They're just doing what I've allowed. Or worse . . . what I've taught." And there it was, the mirror moment I had been waiting for.

Suddenly he wasn't the victim of his job. He was the designer of his leadership. He realized his team was simply reflecting his patterns back to him. When he didn't see accountability in them, it wasn't just their behavior; it was his leadership that gave them permission to stay small.

That was his game-changer. From that day forward, we redefined accountability not as blame, but as *empowerment*. Not as pressure, but as *possibility*. It became his edge. His standard. His power source.

THOUGHT SHIFTER

What Does Accountability Mean to You?

Write these down. No filter. Just your first gut-level answers:

1. Accountability is . . .

_____

_____

_____

_____

2. Accountability feels . . .

_____

_____

_____

_____

_____

3. Accountable people are . . .

_____

_____

_____

_____

_____

4. I am accountable when . . .

_____

_____

_____

_____

_____

This is your leadership mirror. Not to punish, but to reflect and to realign. Because when you get accountability right, when you model it instead of just demanding it, your leadership stops being a performance . . . and starts being a catalyst. This is the kind of leadership the world needs more of. And this is the kind of leadership you were born for.

BONUS EXERCISE

The Energy Reset: Use What Moves You

During one of our sessions, I gave Steven an exercise built around a song that spoke to his soul. His song was called "Right Here Right Now" by my dear friend Melissa Lewis. It was personal. It was grounding. And it worked for him.

We all know music is personal, and that's why it speaks to the soul. The key isn't the song. The key is the shift. So instead of prescribing a specific track, I'm inviting you to create your own version of the tool I gave Steven. Heck, create your own playlist for that matter.

When you're spiraling, disconnected, or caught in emotional chaos, you don't need a new planner. You need a pause. Here's how to take one:

Step 1: Find Your Anchor Song

Pick a song that grounds you. Something that brings you back to yourself. Could be soulful. Could be instrumental. It could be the beat that gets you in the flow.

Step 2: Drop In

Put on your headphones. Breathe. Close your eyes if you can. Let your body drop into presence.

Step 3: Scan and Name

Ask yourself:

- Where am I holding tension?
- What emotion is living there?
- What fear or frustration is driving this moment?

Step 4: Choose and Shift

Ask:

- What do I want to feel instead?
- What do I want to bring to this next interaction or decision?

Name it.
Write it down.
Say it out loud.
"Right here, right now, I choose [peace, clarity, strength, courage]."
This is how you reset.
This is how you reclaim.
This is how you lead.

CHAPTER 16

· · · · · · · · · ·

ACTION. ACCOUNTABILITY. FOLLOW UP. REPEAT.

By now, you've probably seen what happens when a leader hits the edge and instead of falling off, expands. Now it's your turn. If accountability is the power move of leadership, then action, accountability, follow-up, repeat is the rhythm. It's not a one-time decision. It's a lifestyle. A way of leading. A way of being in relationship with people, performance, and purpose. This is where your leadership gets traction. Because the truth? You can't coach what you don't model. You can't expect follow through if you don't follow up. And you can't build a culture of ownership if you're still rescuing, excusing, or avoiding what needs to be addressed.

Action, accountability, follow-up, repeat is a promise. To your people. To your goals. To your integrity. So if you're ready to stop repeating the cycle of frustration and finally lead with energy that moves mountains, this is where it begins. Let's talk about what happens when leaders stop hoping, stop hinting, and start *following through*. Welcome to the rhythm that transforms teams.

Accountability is a leadership lifestyle. A mindset. A way of being that changes how you speak, how you lead, how you build trust, and how you get results. Let's get one thing straight: Accountability isn't about blame. It's not about pressure. And it damn sure isn't about micromanaging. It's action in motion. Follow up with a purpose. Ownership with teeth.

I don't just teach accountability; I live it. Breathe it. Preach it. Because without it, leadership collapses under good intentions and lost potential. With it? You build a culture where people step up, follow through, and create measurable, repeatable wins.

I have to start by breaking the myth: Accountability isn't something you enforce. It's something you embody and something you model. Your team is watching. They learn more from what you do than what you say. If your team struggles to follow through, show initiative, or own their part, ask yourself: *What are they learning from me?*

The Core Truth: *I Am Accountable to You For Your Success!*

A leader is accountable *first* to the success of their team. If your team isn't doing it, they're not seeing it. If there's no follow up, there's no finish line. And if results keep falling short? Stop preaching accountability. Start practicing it. Let me show you what this looks like in the real world.

THE STORY OF RAJ: FROM 'IT'S ON THEM' TO 'IT STARTS WITH ME'

Raj was 26, fresh into an executive role at a national publishing company. Bright. Ambitious. Ready to prove himself. On paper, he looked like a rising star. He had a direct line to the CEO, a big job to do, and a fresh vision to turn around a division whose subscription numbers were free falling. He had ideas, drive, and charisma. What didn't he have? A real understanding of *accountability*.

In those early sessions, Raj came to coaching fired up with lists, initiatives, and frustration. "I'm holding the line," he said. "But my team just isn't stepping up. They're not owning anything." It was clear he cared. He was passionate. But he was also placing the blame entirely outside of himself. When we dug into his patterns, something started to reveal itself. He wasn't following up. He wasn't asking real questions. He was assuming people "should just know."

And underneath it all, he was exhausted from carrying it all alone. He had fallen into the same trap so many new leaders do: confusing *accountability* with *pressure*. And here's the twist that catches even the most well-meaning leaders off guard: Raj wasn't just pressuring himself; he was unknowingly manipulating accountability with *hyped-up language* that sounded urgent but landed weak. You've heard it, and maybe even said it: "Hey, we really need to get this done."

"Let's make a plan." "Someone needs to own this." Sounds collaborative, right? Sounds motivating? Maybe. But **that language is a leadership smokescreen.** It's vague. It's indirect.

It sounds like a call to action, but it leaves the door wide open for confusion, assumption, and avoidance. Because when you say "we need," without saying *who, when,* or *how,* what your team hears is **"not me."** There's no ownership. No follow-through. And no one feels truly accountable because no one was actually *asked* to be. That realization hit Raj like a brick.

"I thought I was rallying them," he said.

"No," I told him. "You were giving them an out."

We broke it down together. He started listening to his own language, emails, meetings, and hallway conversations. Sure enough, he defaulted to soft group-speak instead of clear direction. We rewired the pattern. Instead of "Let's come up with a plan," he practiced: **"Cynthia, I'd like you to draft a plan for this by Friday. Let's review it together on Monday and show me what you advise."**

"Someone should own this" became: **"DeShawn, I think you're the best person to lead this. Can I count on you to take point and to get with me in two weeks to present your ideas?"**

Accountability and follow up stopped being implied. They became explicit. Clear. Energizing. Shared. And guess what happened next? People stepped up. Because people *want* clarity; they *want* to lead. They just need a leader who stops hiding behind polite language and starts drawing lines worth showing up for. That was the game changer for Raj. He stopped trying to *motivate* his team with fluff hype talk, and he started *activating* them with clarity.

And that's when the performance flipped. Raj realized his own role had been the breakdown; he'd been over-functioning, fixing things instead of addressing the root, and unintentionally teaching his team to wait on him rather than lead with him. He was cracked open, and from there, we were able to rebuild his relationship with accountability, not as a tool to *get people to perform*, but as a way of *showing up with consistency, clarity, and care*. Raj stopped seeing accountability as something to enforce, and he started seeing it as something to embody.

And the biggest shift? He made *follow up* non-negotiable. Every meeting ended with "takeaway" action steps, meaning those were what the next meeting started with. Every goal was tied to a date. Every commitment had a revisit point. Not to micromanage, but to *model* what accountability looks and feels like when it's rooted in integrity, not fear. Of course, it wasn't always clean. He had moments where the old habits kicked in, where he wanted to blame, where he wanted to fix. But instead of spiraling, Raj got curious. He took ownership. He coached himself in real time. And it worked.

Within six months, Raj's team was outperforming every other division. Subscription growth hit thirty-one percent. Engagement soared. People showed up earlier, spoke up more, and owned more than ever. He was sleeping better, delegating better, and *leading* better. Raj didn't just win executive of the year at the end-of-year awards ceremony. He walked across the stage in that designer suit, ten pounds lighter, exactly as he had envisioned in our first session. But more than that, he walked across with *freedom*. Not just from the pressure—from the false idea that accountability is something you enforce on others,

He had learned the truth: **Accountability isn't a punishment. It's a way of being.** It's ownership in motion. It's leadership in alignment. And it starts with you. That's what Raj modeled. That's what multiplied. That's what won. And that? Is the ripple that changes everything.

THE EXPANSION MODEL OF ACCOUNTABILITY

We break it down like this: **Action. Accountability. Follow Up. Repeat.**

It's not just a framework, it's a rhythm. A culture. A way to breathe life into your leadership.

- **Action:** What did you commit to doing?
- **Accountability:** Did you do it? Who's holding space for your success?
- **Follow Up:** What's the check-in rhythm? What's working? What's stuck? What's next?
- **Repeat:** Because consistency compounds results.

When you install this rhythm into your leadership, everything changes. Meetings have purpose. Goals have traction. People show up because they feel seen, heard, and supported.

This isn't babysitting. This is high-performance leadership. It's what moves teams from talk to traction.

THOUGHT SHIFTER

Build Your Accountability Muscle

Grab your journal or your favorite voice memo app and reflect:

1. What's one commitment I've been avoiding follow up on?

_____

_____

_____

_____

_____

_____

2. Where am I modeling inconsistent accountability to my team?

_____

_____

_____

_____

_____

3. Who's holding me accountable? And am I letting them?

_____

_____

_____

_____

_____

4. What's one new follow-up rhythm I can implement this week?

_____

_____

_____

_____

_____

5. Where can I make accountability visible, empowering, and non-negotiable?

_____

_____

_____

_____

_____

_____

You're Not Just Leading Projects. You're Leading People.

If your team doesn't trust your follow through, they won't trust your direction. If you keep saying, "We'll check back on that" . . . but never do? You're training them not to listen.

Accountability is a reciprocal partnership, not punishment. It's how you become the kind of leader people trust. Follow. And become. This chapter? It's your cue to stop hoping people will show up better . . . and start showing them how. Lead like it matters. Because it does.

FACTOR 3

· · · · · · · · ·

EXPAND IN LOVE—EXPAND IN PRESENCE

Before you can expand the love you experience, you have to expand the love you believe you deserve. Love isn't a finish line. It's a frequency. It's not something you chase; it's something you *allow*, *embody*, and *expand* from the inside out. You're always expanding something in your relationships: trust or doubt. Connection or distance. Possibility or protection. The real question? **What kind of love are you expanding?**

Expanding love doesn't mean hustling to be picked or performing to feel worthy. It means shifting your inner world so the love you give, receive, and live in is *real*, *rooted*, and *expansive*.

In this factor, you'll explore how to:

- Love without losing yourself.
- Spot and shift the beliefs that block deeper connection.
- Move from reaction to intention in your closest relationships.
- Redefine what love really means—*for you*.
- Receive, embody, and expand love in every corner of your life.

You expand love by becoming the space where it lands.

When you're ready, let's love bigger, fuller, and deeper, starting with *you*.

. . . .

CHAPTER 17

LOVE ISN'T MISSING— IT'S WAITING ON YOU

When you stop frantically searching for someone else to hand you love and instead *unlock even a drop of love for yourself,* a funny thing happens: That drop becomes a well. That well becomes a fountain. And that fountain? It becomes the very energy that attracts deeper, healthier, more aligned relationships.

The other night, I found myself at dinner sandwiched between two friends, both deep in their own love trouble. On my left, one friend poked at her pasta and sighed, wishing for a relationship. "I'm so tired of going home to an empty apartment," she said. "Is it too much to ask for someone to share life with?"

Meanwhile, on my right, my other friend stirred the ice in her drink, questioning the relationship she already had. "I know I should be happy . . . but sometimes I feel so alone even when he's right next to me," she confessed. "Is there something wrong with me? Or with us?"

There I was, caught in the middle with a front-row seat to love's bittersweet irony, one person aching to find love and the other unsure if she should keep it. I almost did a spit-take with my soda at the cosmic joke unfolding. Here were two smart, beautiful women, each convinced they had a love deficit. The single friend thought a partner would fill her emptiness; the partnered friend thought leaving hers would fix her unhappiness.

Talk about opposite problems. It was like watching two people on a seesaw, each one thinking the other side has it better. In that moment, I couldn't help but chuckle (with a side of raw compassion) at how we can all be so tricked by our own beliefs about love. The grass isn't just greener on the other side; it's a full technicolor fantasy that none of us can live up to. And yet, we chase it.

Love is an emotion, not a person.

Read that again. Slowly. Love is an emotion, not a person! Love is a feeling. A state of being. *Not* some magical person or missing puzzle piece that, once found, makes everything perfect.

But oh man, do we get this twisted.

We grow up believing that love lives "out there." In the crush who doesn't know we exist. In the Tinder match we haven't met yet. In the partner we hope will finally start doing the dishes without being asked. We're taught to treat love like it's a thing to get or lose. A goal. A reward. A fix. A solution.

That night at dinner, both of my friends had unknowingly handed over the keys to their happiness. One to an imaginary future partner. One to the partner sitting next to her. Neither of them realized that what they were truly aching for wasn't a person—it was a *feeling* they thought only someone else could give them.

Let's get real. It's band-aid ripping time. *No other person can give you the love you refuse to give yourself.* That one sentence might rattle your soul, but let it. Because here's what it really means: You could meet the kindest, most emotionally available human on the planet, and it still wouldn't be enough *if* you keep rejecting your own worth on the inside. It's like trying to quench your thirst with a cracked glass. No matter how much love gets poured in, it leaks right out through the fractures you haven't sealed. You end up starving in the middle of a feast, wondering why nothing satisfies. Not because love isn't available, but because you've been wired to believe it has to come from some-one else.

We carry around subconscious stories about love that sabotage us at every turn. Maybe you secretly believe you're unworthy of love unless someone validates you. Maybe you think love always ends in pain, so you never let yourself fully receive it. Maybe love, to you, has always been conditional, something you earn by being "good enough," "low maintenance," or "not too much." These beliefs are like invisible puppeteers, twisting our expectations, our behaviors, and our capacity to actually *feel* love even when it's right in front of us.

My single friend had a subconscious belief that being single meant being incomplete.

My coupled friend had a belief that being in love meant being smothered or losing herself.

Neither belief was true. But both were running the show.

Think on these things:

- What if love isn't something you *hunt down* or *wait for*, but something you *recognize and release from within yourself?*
- What if the love you've been looking for "out there" has been quietly inside you all along, just waiting for you to notice it?
- What part of yourself have you been withholding from love because you thought someone else had to give it to you first?

Not gonna lie, this might change everything: You are already whole. Already worthy. Already loved. Whether you're single, married, divorced, or "it's complicated," love is not missing; it's just waiting for you to *see* it again.

LET'S CALL THIS WHAT IT IS: A WAKE-UP CALL.

This part of the book isn't about dating strategies or communication hacks. This is about *returning* to the love that's already in you and expanding it.

And let me be clear: We're not talking woo-woo fluff about self love in a bubble bath (though if that's your thing, pour the champagne and enjoy it). We're talking real, unshakable, expansive love, the kind that wakes you up at 2 a.m. and says, "You don't have to abandon yourself anymore." Forget the surface-level affirmations. You're experiencing root-level revolution. It's about building an internal foundation so fierce and so grounded that no external circumstances—not your relationship status, not your past heartbreak, not even your current chaos—can shake who you know yourself to be. *Because if expansion is the heartbeat of this book, then love is the soul of it.* Not the clingy kind. Not dependency disguised as devotion. Not the fantasy fix or fairytale illusion we've been sold. But the kind that roots you in truth and dares you to stay there, fully seen, fully felt, fully you. Love as in radical presence, unshakable truth, and full-bodied self acceptance. That's the kind of love that expands you. It makes you bigger, not smaller. It calls you to the front of your own life. Whether you're single, partnered, in transition, or somewhere in the "what the hell is happening?" stage, this kind of love lets you hold it all with grace and fire. It's the kind of love that becomes the launch pad for everything else. Because when you stop outsourcing your worth and start owning your love, everything changes.

And let's be real. What we're talking about isn't just romantic love. It's the love that shapes how you see the world, treat yourself, and walk through a room. It's how you show up in the hard conversations, the quiet mornings, the messy middles.

The way you do love, with yourself, your work, your people, is the same way you do expansion. It's the same energy. And the quality of that love? It determines the size of your life. So no matter where you are on the relationship map—heartbroken, hopeful, healing, or happily partnered—consider this your portal. Your permission slip. Your sacred invitation to stop waiting for love to come find you and start activating it, living it, being it. Because love isn't a destination; it's your damn frequency. Loving yourself deeply turns your relationships into a reflection of that, not a substitute for it. Waking up to love means seeing it as a state of being, not a status to check off on a form. It's reclaiming the parts of yourself that got lost in old relationships. It's rewriting the stories you've carried about love. And it's becoming the version of you that loves from wholeness, not from fear, pressure, or performance. Because when you do that, your entire experience of love changes. Not because someone else swoops in to save you, but because you stop waiting to be saved. You show up. You open. You expand.

A LOVE LETTER TO THE YOU THAT FORGOT

You don't have to do more, be more, or find someone to finally feel it.

You are love. Already. And the moment you choose to believe that, even just a little, is the moment you start expanding in a way no partner, relationship status, or dating app could ever replicate. Are you ready? Let's expand in love.

THOUGHT SHIFTER

Reclaim the Love Within

This is your inner invitation. Take a few minutes with each question. Let them be a mirror, not a measuring stick.

1. What belief about love have I been carrying that no longer serves me?

_____

_____

_____

_____

_____

2. Where have I been outsourcing my sense of worth or waiting for someone else to make me feel whole?

_____

_____

_____

3. What does love feel like in my body when I'm giving it to *myself* and not earning it from someone else?

_____

_____

_____

4. How would my relationships shift if I stopped chasing love and started embodying it?

_____

_____

_____

5. What's one daily practice I can commit to that helps me connect to love within, right here, right now?

_____

_____

_____

Love is not something to get. It's something you *give* to yourself first, so that every other kind of love flows from overflow, not emptiness.

CHAPTER 18

. . . .

LOVING WITHOUT LOSING YOURSELF

We don't lose ourselves in love overnight. It starts subtly. Quietly. A "Sure, I'll skip that thing I love just this once."

A "No big deal; I'll wait to share what I really feel."

A "Maybe I am too much."

Bit by bit, we trade parts of ourselves, our opinions, our routines, and our passions for the illusion of harmony. We shrink our voice to avoid conflict. We downplay our needs to keep the peace. We over function to prove we're lovable. And then one day, we look in the mirror and ask, "Wait . . . where did I go?"

That's what this chapter is about. This isn't about the thrill of falling or the sting of heartbreak. It's about the quiet erosion that happens in the middle, the part no one talks about. And the bold act of reclaiming who you are while staying connected, not by pulling away, but by rooting deeper into yourself.

Take Harper, for example.

When she first started dating Jordan, she was electric. She wore bold lipstick, planned impromptu road trips, and hosted wine nights where her laugh could fill a room. But over time, small shifts began to creep in.

He teased her once about being "too loud," so she started holding back her jokes. He rolled his eyes when she brought up her business idea, so she stopped talking about it. He didn't love her friends, so she saw them less. Nothing dramatic. Nothing cruel. Just quiet, steady choices to avoid friction, each one costing her a little piece of herself.

By the time she reached out to me, she wasn't in a toxic relationship . . . she was in a ghost version of her own life. Still in love but hollow. Functioning but disconnected. She couldn't point to the moment she disappeared, only that she did.

WHY WE DISAPPEAR

The world doesn't teach us to love with boundaries. It teaches us to merge. To please. To perform. To prioritize "we" at the expense of "me." Especially for women, especially in caregiving roles, especially when we've been praised for being selfless. But love that costs you *you* is not love. It's a transaction. It's a performance. And it's not sustainable. You were not made to shape shift to be chosen. You were not meant to play small to keep someone else comfortable. You were never meant to trade your wholeness for belonging.

And yet . . . most of us have all done it. We twist ourselves into versions of "easy to love." We stop sharing our truth if it might rock the boat. We stop dancing, creating, laughing, resting, or dreaming like we used to. Not because we don't love ourselves, but because somewhere along the line, we believed love only works when we're easier, quieter, less *us*.

Like Elena.

She was the glue in every relationship, the one who remembered birthdays, stayed up late listening, and made space for everyone else's chaos. Her boyfriend once called her "the calm in the storm," and she wore that title like a badge. But over time, being *the calm* meant swallowing her feelings when plans changed. It meant not asking for help when she was overwhelmed. It meant downplaying her joy when he was stressed. She told herself she was being supportive. That she was "stronger." That needing less made her easier to love.

But one day, after yet another dinner where she listened and nodded and made sure *he* felt better, she got into her car and realized she couldn't remember the last time she said how *she* really felt. Not even to herself.

That's how disappearance happens. Slowly. Quietly. Dressed up as love.

THE RELATIONSHIP AUDIT THAT CHANGES EVERYTHING

Suppose you've ever felt that knot in your stomach, wondering, *"Why do I feel so distant from myself in this relationship?"* You're not alone. Let's do something right now, not just in your head. Grab a notebook, open a voice memo, or speak this aloud in the mirror. Yes, *really*. Let this be a moment with yourself.

Start here:

- When was the last time I felt most like *me*?
- What was I doing?
- How did I speak? Move? Dress? Dream?
- What lit me up?
- What made me laugh like a total dork, unfiltered and full-body?

Now go deeper:

- Are those things still present in my life today?
- If not, when did they start to fade?
- And why?
- •What version of me have I quietly stopped bringing to the table?

That gap you feel? It's not always about your partner. Sometimes it's about the version of you that you stopped bringing to the table.

Sometimes it's about the quiet agreements you made to disconnect from your own magic. Here's what most people won't say out loud . . . *no healthy love asks you to mute your joy.*

Hold on to what just came up.

I want to tell you a story, and after you hear it, we'll revisit what you just uncovered and see if anything shifts.

SIENNA'S AWAKENING

Sienna came to me six months into her marriage, already unraveling. On the outside, she and Alex had it all. They were the golden couple. But inside, Sienna felt invisible.

"I don't know what's wrong with me," she said, twisting a bracelet around her wrist. "I love him. But I don't feel like myself anymore."

We traced it back—the gradual fade.

Sienna used to paint, blast music, and dance while cooking. She also used to laugh until she snorted and make up stories about strangers in restaurants just for fun.

But somewhere between trying to "be a good wife" and avoid conflict, she stopped.

She'd hear Alex make a joke that landed sideways, but she'd stay silent.

She'd want to spend a weekend with her friends but worry he'd feel left out.

She skipped her art classes because "they were expensive" and "not essential."

She told herself she was just adjusting. But really? She was disappearing.

What hit her hardest was this: Alex fell in love with the woman who danced in the kitchen and told wild stories. The more she tried to be "right" for him, the less of herself she brought to the relationship. And they both felt it.

In one session, I asked her, "What if your return to joy is the most loving thing you could do for your marriage?"

She went stiff and then cried. It was not long before she started painting again—sunflowers, oceans, abstract bursts of color that looked like freedom—just to bring it to life visually and emotionally. She started laughing more. She spoke up more, softly at first, then more confidently. She didn't blame Alex. She didn't shame herself. She just recentered.

And Alex? He noticed. He didn't feel threatened. He felt *closer.*

Because when Sienna came home to herself, the space between them finally felt real again. Alive. Not because she contorted to stay in love, but because she expanded and brought love with her.

LOVING WITHOUT LOSING: THE EXPANSION PRACTICE

Now pause. Go back to what you just wrote. Look at those answers again, or speak them again if you went verbal.

WHAT DO YOU NOTICE NOW THAT YOU'VE HEARD SIENNA'S STORY?

Would you add anything?

Did anything surprise you about what you remembered or what you forgot?

What's one part of your joy, rhythm, or magic that deserves to return *now?*

If you've felt yourself fade, this is your call-back. Real love doesn't ask for less of you; it makes space for all of you. You were never meant to whisper in your own life. So don't wait for someone else to turn the volume back up. This is your cue.

TRY THIS SELF-AUDIT

1. What part of me have I muted in the name of keeping the peace?

---

2. Where have I over-functioned or over-given in hopes of being loved more?

---

3. What activities, people, or practices reconnect me with me?

---

4. What's one small way I can return to myself this week?

---

5. If love is expansion, what version of myself is love inviting me back to?

_____

_____

_____

_____

Let this be your turning point. Not a breakup. Not a blow-up. A _reclaiming_. You don't have to choose between love and yourself. You don't have to dilute your joy to stay connected. The right love? It wants your fullness. And if you're already in a relationship where you've started to disappear, maybe the most radical act of love you can make isn't walking away. **It's coming back to you.** Speak. Move. Laugh. Create. Rebuild your rhythm. Not to leave the relationship . . . but to resurrect the one you're in. Because the more you come home to yourself, the more love has a home to live in, too.

THOUGHT SHIFTER

Reclaiming Your Center

1. When did I feel most like _me_ in love?

_____

_____

_____

2. What pieces of myself have I quietly tucked away?

_____

_____

_____

3. Where am I confusing peace with people-pleasing?

_____

_____

_____

_____

4. How can I invite more *me* into my relationship(s)?

_____

_____

_____

_____

5. What would it feel like to be fully loved *as I am,* not as I perform?

_____

_____

_____

_____

This isn't just self love. This is soul return. And the ones who love you most? They'll cheer when you rise.

CHAPTER 19

SEEING YOUR PARTNER WITH NEW EYES

BREAKING THE SUBCONSCIOUS LOVE LOOP THAT KEEPS YOU STUCK

It didn't start with a fight. It started with a feeling. This one might rattle your comfort zone . . . because love isn't just long walks, shared playlists, and "date night" Instagram stories. Love is layered. It's nuanced. It's messy. And sometimes? It's an echo of the stories we've carried since childhood. We think we're choosing a partner based on what we want. But more often than not, we're reacting to what we lacked, feared, or normalized. And unless we shine a light on that subconscious wiring, we'll find ourselves in loops we didn't even know we built.

MEET MILLIE AND ROBERT

Eight years into their marriage. Two kids. Thriving careers. A life that looked "complete" on paper, but something wasn't syncing.

Millie came to me first. She was a SVP at a manufacturing company, driven, smart, and high-functioning. A woman who made room for everyone . . . except herself.

"I'm exhausted, but I don't know how to stop," she said in our first session. "There's always something: homework, dinner, work emails, someone needing something. I love my life, but I feel invisible in it."

Then Robert came in. Let's just say . . . he didn't walk in with a gratitude journal. His frustration came out sideways. First as silence. Then as sarcasm. And finally, the gut-punch. One night, sitting over takeout, both of them worn down, eyes heavy, he hit her with: "Do you even *see* me anymore? You put the kids, work, and everyone before me. I feel like a background prop in my own marriage."

Millie froze. Her eyes welled. "Are you serious right now? I am holding everything together, and you think *you're* invisible?"

What followed wasn't just an argument. It was a cracking open. And underneath the tension was something far deeper: years of unspoken needs, invisible expectations, and subconscious love loops driving the relationship.

Robert grew up with a mother who did everything, sometimes beautifully, sometimes to the point of enabling. She anticipated every need, folded every sock, and finished every sentence. To him, love meant caretaking, physical presence, and being the center of someone else's orbit.

But Robert didn't want to marry his mother. He wanted adventure. Spark. Independence. That's what drew him to Millie in the first place. She lit up rooms. She had her own dreams. She wasn't defined by him.

Here's the twist: The very thing that once attracted him, her independence, eventually triggered the wound he'd never addressed. Because deep down, his subconscious still craved the kind of attention that looked like being cared for.

Millie? She learned to survive by being the strong one. The doer. Her love language was acts of service. Handle the tasks. Keep the machine running. That's how she proved love. But Robert wasn't needing efficiency, he was starving for emotional prioritization.

Their hearts meant well, but their energy told a different story. They were stuck in subconscious loops, each speaking a language the other couldn't decode. Their frequencies couldn't align. It was like try-ing to tune into two different radio stations at once—all static, no connection. They were trapped in patterns shaped by upbringing, past pain, and unspoken beliefs. Expectations that neither of them could fully name, yet that both were being held accountable to.

Millie believed:

- If I'm doing everything, I'm showing love.
- If I stop, everything will fall apart.
- Needing help means I'm failing.

Robert believed:

- If I'm not prioritized, I'm not loved.
- If you loved me, you'd just know.
- If I speak up, I'm being ungrateful.

These beliefs were never voiced. Just felt. Just acted out.

Unspoken, but deeply felt. Acted out . . . until one day, every-thing cracked.

BREAKING THE LOOP: THE POWER OF AWARENESS

In coaching, we unpacked it. Slowly. With compassion.

Millie realized her constant busyness wasn't just burnout; it was a shield, a way to prove her worth without needing to be vulnera-ble. She hadn't just disconnected from Robert; she had disconnected from herself.

Robert came to understand that his expectations were rooted in a childhood version of love that no longer served him. He wasn't seeking partnership; he was unknowingly seeking parenting. That shift was game changing.

Together, they began to rebuild, not from performance, but from presence.

What That Looked Like:

- **Intentional Connection**: fifteen-minute check-ins twice a week. No kids. No phones. No agenda. Just honesty.
- **Mutual Curiosity**: They started asking, "What's one thing you need from me this week to feel supported?"
- **Awareness Pauses**: "Is this reaction about now? Or is it an old story playing out?"
- **Celebrating Efforts**: Every shift was acknowledged. No act is too small. No step unworthy of being seen.

And most importantly? They began to see each other with new eyes. Not through the lens of lack. Not through the fog of assumption. But through the truth of what was still possible.

Remember your RAS (reticular activating system)? We talked about it back in Agreement 1 and again in Chapter 5. It's the mental filter in your brain that only lets in what you already believe or expect. It's not just neuroscience; it's your expansion gatekeeper. Millie's RAS was tuned to everything she wasn't doing. Robert's was tuned to everywhere he wasn't being prioritized.

So we trained a new filter. They started noticing:

- Moments of generosity
- Invitations for connection
- Shared wins
- Humor in the chaos
- Efforts over outcomes

And that changed everything. Because what you focus on in love? It becomes what you find.

YOUR TURN

If you're in a relationship (or reflecting on a past one), try asking yourself:

- What stories about love did I inherit? How are they still showing up?
- Where might I be interpreting actions through my fears instead of their intent?
- What am I expecting my partner to "just know"?
- What would change if I looked at them with new eyes right now?

THOUGHT SHIFTER

New Eyes, New Love

1. What love story am I subconsciously reenacting?

_____

_____

_____

_____

2. Where am I assuming intent without seeking clarity?

_____

_____

_____

_____

_____

3. What does my partner already do that shows love—even if it's not my language?

_____

_____

_____

_____

_____

4. What's one new way I could choose to see them this week?

_____

_____

_____

_____

5. How can I shift my RAS to notice what's working?

_____

_____

_____

_____

Love doesn't require perfect harmony all the time. Sometimes love is a decision to break the loop. To update the filter. To stop scanning for what's wrong and start noticing what's beautiful.

That's what Millie and Robert did.

And maybe, just maybe, that's where your expansion in love begins, too.

. . . .

CHAPTER 20

LOVE, DEFINED—A MIRROR FOR THE HEART

Let's pause for a second.

We've been talking about love, not the Hallmark-card version or the rom-com montage, but real love. The kind that stretches you. That breaks your old patterns. That makes you look inward and ask, "What the hell am I even doing here?"

But before we go any further in this section of the book, I want you to check something really important: **What do you *actually* believe about love?**

Not what you *want* to believe. Not what you *post* about. Not what you *hope* is true one day. I'm talking about the beliefs that live under the surface. The ones that are shaping every single relationship you have. The ones that tell your brain what to focus on. The ones that whisper behind the scenes of your choices, your reactions, and your patterns.

Because if you don't know what those beliefs are . . . you might just be reenacting someone else's definition of love—your parents', your ex's, your third-grade crush's, your trauma's—without even realizing it. And that? That's not expansion. That's repetition.

So let's get honest. Let's get curious. Let's get *free*.

Unveiling subconscious beliefs about love is not a fluffy quiz or a journal prompt that's gonna gather dust in a notebook. This is a *mirror*.

A flashlight. These beliefs are why you have the results you have, no matter what those are. You authored them, and your beliefs are the key to the door of awareness to change them if you want to.

You will need to go all in. I remember doing this; I have done several renditions in my lifetime. Love for me was so clouded, and seeing through my misconceptions was nearly impossible, so step by step was my path—one belief at a time. The first belief was even to believe the exercise mattered. I didn't really have anyone teach me this; I just realized it's what I did after permitting myself to seek my subconscious thoughts. I do that often now with many things I feel "stuckness" around. Yep, when you're stuck, that is where you will find it, and then a trigger will tell you you are stuck. It's a pretty clear pattern that is actually very supportive for me.

Here is how it works:

Answer each prompt one at a time with your **first raw instinct.** Don't overthink it. Can't stress this enough. Your logic will try to mask and override your very first thought, so do you best to "go there." Don't justify it. Just write. Take **thirty to forty-five seconds** per question. Capture a *word or two*. Maybe a sentence. That's it. You can come back and unpack more later, but for now, we're just surfacing the stuff that lives deep.

Here we go:

1. Love is . . .
2. People who have love in their life . . .
3. People who give a lot of love to others are . . .
4. When I love, I receive or experience . . .
5. I feel _____ when I hear or use the word love.
6. I am lovable when . . .
7. I learned how to love from . . .
8. When they showed me love, they . . .
9. Because of them, I give love to others by . . .
10. My current definition of love is . . .

SO . . . WHAT NOW?

You just revealed your emotional operating system. Those raw patterns that were running in the background? Now they're pulled to the surface. Look at them, not with judgment, but with curiosity. Ask yourself:

Where did these beliefs come from?

Which ones actually feel true to me now?

Which ones feel limiting, outdated, or rooted in fear?

What beliefs do I want to expand into moving forward?

Truth moment. No filters, no fluff. Your subconscious beliefs about love are the lens shaping every connection you have. The only way to shift your patterns? Change the lens. We're not here to "fix" you. We're here to meet you. You're not here to earn love. You're here to remember it's already yours. So as we move forward in this book, I want you to carry one truth with you: *My love story is not on repeat. It's being rewritten. By me. Right now.* And babe, if that's not expansion? I don't know what is.

THOUGHT SHIFTER

Simple—Do the above when you are ready.

CHAPTER 21

· · · · · · · · · ·

LOVE REDEFINED

THE BELIEFS THAT BLOCK US

This isn't just another journal prompt chapter. This is a deep dive into what's *really* running the show in your love life and how to flip the script once and for all.

Let me be clear: If you skimmed past the "What Is Love?" exercise in Chapter 22 thinking, *Yeah, yeah, I've done stuff like this before*, I urge you to go back and do it when you're truly ready. Not because it's cute or trendy, but because *knowing your beliefs* is how you change your results. Period. Your subconscious beliefs about love are shaping everything from how you choose partners to how you respond to conflict to how much love you're willing to receive.

Let's get honest: If you've been through heartbreak, betrayal, abandonment, or trauma and never really released it, your definition of love might be blocking you from fully receiving it. Love might feel like danger. Or disappointment. Or work. You might say you want it, but deep down, your body's bracing for pain. And here's the kicker: *That's not love's fault.* That's your subconscious, still trying to protect you. It runs the show from behind the curtain, and most people don't even know the script they're living by.

Let me tell you what changed my life and what I teach every single day: **There are only two core emotional roots to everything you feel, do, say, or attract in your life.**

Love. And fear.

That's it. Everything else—joy, resentment, confidence, shame, peace, discouragement, anxiety—is just a branch off one of those two roots.

Imagine a spectrum:

FEAR ————————————————— LOVE

Everything you believe, everything you expand, sits somewhere on that line. The closer you are to fear, the more life feels tight, heavy, and reactive, and you are expanding all of those things. The closer you are to love, the more life feels open, expansive, creative, and calm, and yes, you are expanding those things.

Now, take that framework and apply it to your beliefs about love.

If, deep down, you believe love equals sacrifice, exhaustion, abandonment, or loss of freedom, then no matter how many positive affirmations you tape to your mirror, your subconscious will keep sabotaging your relationships. It's not punishment. It's programming.

You can't expand love in its richest form if you haven't redefined it.

And that brings me to Jovelle.

She didn't come crying. She didn't collapse in heartbreak. She showed up to her sessions in the way many of my most accomplished clients do—sharp, armored, and slightly skeptical. But underneath the control? There was a story begging to be rewritten.

Jovelle grew up in a world full of contradictions. Her parents divorced when she was eight, and everything after that became about strategy, not sentiment. She stayed with her mom; her two older brothers moved in with their dad. The idea was "logical." Boys need a man's influence. Girls need their mom. Weekend rotations were established. On paper, the plan was fair. Emotionally? It was a fracture she never quite recovered from.

Jovelle's father never remarried; he just shuffled through girlfriends like chapters in a book he didn't want to finish. Her mother married three more times. None of those marriages were stable. Love looked more like negotiation and survival than safety.

And those two brothers? One was a rising athlete, the kind who drew attention without trying. The other was a quiet soul, artistic and deeply empathetic. Jovelle watched one perform for approval and the other withdraw for protection. She learned from both and then chose a different path entirely.

Education became her escape. Her ticket. Her currency.

She decided early: *If I can earn my way, I'll never have to rely on anyone. Especially not a man.*

And though her brothers had protected her, taught her, and loved her the best they could, she still coded male dependence as dangerous. Because in her house, the men left or were detached and disappointed. So while she loved her brothers deeply, she also silently vowed to never need anyone the way she saw her mother need . . . and fall.

She hustled. And that hustle, from all appearances, worked for her. Until it didn't.

She earned a full-ride academic scholarship. She clawed her way into law. She didn't just build a life; she built an empire. And by fifty, She had it all.

Top attorney at a firm she founded. Financially untouchable. everything. Jet-setting. Respected. Untouchable. But there was one problem: She was lonely as hell. She didn't call it that at first. She called it "tired," "disconnected," or "needing a break." But deep down, she felt hollow. And the moment that cracked her open?

An employee quit. Not just any employee, but her prize, the faithful one, needed to do what you do employee. Her ride-or-die employee. Also surprisingly, it was not for more money, not for prestige. They said, "You don't see us. You don't make work feel human. And honestly? I want a life."

That one landed like a gut punch. Because it wasn't just work. It was everywhere. Her brothers had grown distant. Her dating life? Nonexistent. Her holidays? Spent alone. Not because she didn't have options, but because she didn't want to deal with the energy of pretending. Suddenly she realized she hadn't built a life; she'd built a fortress.

Enter our first session.

She wasn't warm. She wasn't fragile. She was calculating. And powerful. And exhausted. And somewhere in her eyes, I saw the glimmer of someone ready to shift. I asked her to do one thing: you guessed it, the "What Is Love?" exercise. Simple. Fast. Gut answers only. And she obliged.

"Love is . . ."

"Transactional."

"People who have love . . ."

"Have someone they trust. But trust is earned, not given."

"When I love, I get . . ."

"Exposed. Vulnerable. That's why I don't do it."

There it was: Walls up. Heart armored. And not a single word about joy, presence, or safety.

So I flipped it.

"If love weren't a risk . . . if love were an energy, not a transaction . . . what would it be?"

She paused. She closed her eyes. Then slowly: "Love is . . . security. And trust. And ease." And that was it. The first honest breath she'd taken in years. Not because she changed overnight. But because she was willing to *question the script.*

For her entire life, Jovelle had been expanding transactions. Now? She was expanding connection, the kind that actually fuels growth. She didn't leave her job. She didn't dive into therapy marathons or dismantle her life overnight. She started with smaller, more radical acts: She looked her assistant in the eye and asked, "How are you really doing today?" She stopped replying to every message with a bullet-pointed task list and started adding, "Thank you, I appreciate this." She began ending meetings by asking her team what *they* needed instead of just by telling them what needed to be done. She called her brothers, not with an agenda, but with presence. She let the conversations meander. She listened. She laughed. She let silence be okay. And maybe most importantly, she started checking in with herself. At the end of each day, she asked, "Did I connect today? Or just perform?" That was her turning point. Not some grand gesture, but a return to humanity. One intentional moment at a time.

Now, I'm inviting you to do the same.

YOUR TURN: REDEFINE LOVE

1. If love weren't a risk . . . if love were an energy, not a transaction, what would it be?
2. What do people actually have when they have love in their lives?
3. What do people who give a lot of love to others receive in return?
4. When I love, I get . . .
5. If love were an *inside job*—if it started with you—what would love be?

Now breathe. Look at your answers. What did you write? Is love something outside of you? Is it something someone has to give? Is it something you chase? Or something you allow? Because that right there? That's your script. And if it's not working for you, you get to redefine it and rewrite it. You don't need to wait for another heartbreak. You don't need permission. You need awareness. And courage.

Here is what you can walk away with:

You don't chase love. You expand it.
You don't earn love. You embody it.
Love isn't out there waiting to be handed to you.
Love is in you, waiting to be claimed.

And the moment you start living like that's true? Everything changes.

Jovelle's transformation didn't happen in a single "aha" moment. It was a layered unfolding. It took coaching. Some therapy. A whole lot of reflection. And an unexpected coffee conversation with a friend who saw something she couldn't yet see in herself.

It was Cindy Anne, her longtime gym buddy, who first cracked the door open. Not with a lecture. Not with a to-do list. But with one grounded, no-nonsense truth: "People want to feel seen. Not just paid."

That line hit Jovelle like a clean jab to the gut. Not because it was revolutionary, but because deep down, she knew she had stopped seeing people. And more painfully . . . she'd stopped seeing herself. She looked across the table and said, "So what? You just give them feelings instead of bonuses?"

Cindy Anne didn't flinch. "No. I give them both. But the bonus means nothing if they feel invisible. You can't throw money at disconnection and expect it to feel like you value them."

Then she leaned in, softened just enough to land it: "You're brilliant, Jo. But you're guarded. You don't trust connection because somewhere along the way, you decided love and all that stuff was a distraction. Love isn't the problem. The problem is how you've been taught to guard against it. Love, for yourself, for this life, *is* the expansion."

That was the day everything changed.

Jovelle reached out to me after Cindy Anne referred her. She was skeptical at first, coaching sounded like "that fluffy emotional stuff" she had always dismissed. But she trusted Cindy Anne.

And in that first meeting, we got real. Over the next several sessions, we unpacked why she had built walls around herself. We examined why she believed love was a distraction, not an expansion. We uncovered the patterns she had repeated in every area of her life. And then? We redefined what she was expanding because that was the real issue.

Jovelle had spent decades expanding transactions. Now, she was expanding relationships, first with herself and then with others—one relationship, one conversation, one step at a time.

THOUGHT SHIFTER

Redefining the Love You Expand

Sit with this. Don't just read it; feel it. Let this be a turning point for awareness.

Journal or reflect on the following:

1. What am I expanding right now: connection or control?

_____

_____

_____

_____

2. Where have I mistaken love for obligation, transaction, or performance?

_____

_____

_____

_____

_____

3. What old belief about love am I ready to release?

_____

_____

_____

_____

4. Who in my life actually *sees* me? Who have I kept walled out?

_____

_____

_____

_____

5. If love were safe, steady, and expansive . . . how would I show up differently?

_____

_____

_____

_____

Love isn't something you chase, earn, or beg for. It's something you expand from within; the more you trust it, the more it flows. It's not waiting in someone else's hands. It's waiting in *you*. Love is limitless if you let it be. Love is abundant if you stop blocking it. Love is expansive when you finally expand into it. So the question isn't "where is love?" The question is "what am I expanding?" Because love isn't missing. It's waiting. And now?

It's your move.

· · · · · · · · · ·

CHAPTER 22

YOUR BELIEF IS SHOWING— IT'S ALL EXPANDING, EVEN THE B.S.

Every thought you have? Yours.
Every emotion you feel? Also yours.
Every action you take? Your choice.
Every belief you hold? Yours—*until it isn't*.

Let me show you what I mean. A client once told me she had "bad luck with love." Said it like it was a zodiac sign. Every relationship? Chaos. The good ones bored her. The unavailable ones lit her up. "I don't know why this keeps happening," she said. "I do the work. I try to stay open. I want love." So I asked her, "What do you believe about love, *really*?" She paused, thought for a second, then said, "I guess I believe love is hard. It's messy. It hurts."

Bingo. That belief? Running the whole damn show.

She didn't even know she was expanding the very thing she said she didn't want. Because what you believe *quietly*, you expand *loudly*. And unless you stop and look at what's actually running in the background of your mind, you'll keep creating the same loop . . . just with different faces.

That's the thing about expansion: It's not sentimental. It's not selective. It doesn't pause to check if you're aligned or even paying attention. **Expansion is neutral.** It doesn't give a damn what you do with it; it just is. It's the universal law of existence. An unstoppable force like the ever-expanding universe, infinite numbers, or your unread emails. No matter how many you delete, more just keep showing up. Or that pile of laundry that regenerates like it's on a mission from the underworld.

That's the thing about expansion: It doesn't stop. It doesn't pause to check if you're ready, aligned, or even paying attention. Expansion keeps expanding. Whether it's your potential, problems, clarity, or chaos, it grows whatever you feed it. Expansion doesn't care if you focus on your purpose or pain. It'll grow whatever you give it. And that? That's both terrifying or empowering. You get to pick.

This book is about expansion, yes. But not just the kind that sparkles on Instagram with mantras, manifesting, and "look at me now" glow ups. I'm talking about the gritty kind. The kind that calls your bluff. The kind that says, "Hey babe, you keep feeding this belief, so guess what? It's growing." Whether that belief is aligned or distorted, empowering or limiting, expansion doesn't play favorites. It grows your truth or your illusion. Your power or your pain. Your vision or your avoidance. It's neutral. Which means the responsibility? It's yours.

If you've been reading this book and wondering why certain patterns just won't break . . . why the same emotional loops show up in your relationships, your work, your health, your damn inbox? It's probably because you haven't gotten curious enough about what you're unconsciously feeding. So, before we go deeper, it's time for a pattern interrupt. Because if expansion is your birthright (and it is), then clarity is your damn compass.

Let's clarify something: You don't repeat patterns because you're weak or broken. You repeat them because your subconscious is still feeding them. And one of the sneakiest culprits behind that? A little thing called **parataxic distortion** (yeah, say that three times fast).

It's a fancy term coined by psychiatrist Harry S. Sullivan, but here's the real talk: It's the reason you keep falling for potential instead of reality. It's why you assume someone will *just get you* without actually saying what you need. It's why you chase the emotionally unavailable, because somewhere deep down, you still believe love is supposed to be hard. Parataxic distortion is your brain recycling old pain into new people. It warps your present by projecting your past. Instead of seeing people as they are, you see them as what you *expect* them to be: A savior. A betrayer. A walking red flag dressed up as fate. And unless you see the distortion? You'll keep expanding the illusion.

Picture this: You meet someone new and, bam, they're instantly your "soulmate." But, hold up. Do you really know them? Or are you just seeing what you want to see? That's parataxic distortion in action. Our brains, drawing from past experiences and wishful thinking, create these idealized images, setting us up for a reality check when the person doesn't match our fantasy. Beyond these fantasies, our assumptions, gremlins, and limiting beliefs are the sneaky saboteurs. Shaped by previous experiences, they color how we perceive others. They act as mental shortcuts, helping us navigate social interactions but often leading to misunderstandings. For example, if you've been burned before, you might unfairly judge new people, blocking genuine connections.

HOW YOUR BRAIN SCREWS WITH YOU

Let's play a little game.

Picture a little girl in a pink polka-dot dress with a big white bow in her hair. Got her? Good. Now here's the truth: She's not real. She's a projection, a mashup of memories, beliefs, childhood stories, and brain filters. I assure you, no two people reading this book imagined the exact same girl . . . because they *couldn't.* Maybe she reminded you of your childhood. Perhaps she was a version of you. Maybe she felt familiar or was what you always wanted to be. Some saw sweetness. Some saw loneliness. Some saw hope. Some saw grief.

Enter, again, your reticular activating system (RAS), your brain's built-in bouncer. It filters what gets your attention based on what you already believe is important, dangerous, or familiar.

It constantly scans your environment to find more of what you've already decided matters, even if what "matters" is a story rooted in pain. That's why this matters: It's expansion in action. Your thoughts created that girl, and your emotions gave her meaning, color, shape, and tone.

Your RAS, your subconscious filter, told your brain what to highlight and what to ignore. And if that's true for an imaginary girl in a dress . . . imagine how true it is for your definition of love. If your RAS is tuned to "love is pain," "love is work," or "love never lasts," guess what you're going to notice, attract, and expand? More of that.

Your beliefs matter. That's why clarity is your compass. Your brain isn't showing you the truth; it's showing you what it *thinks* you want to see. And if you don't interrupt that?

You'll keep mistaking your patterns for reality . . . instead of seeing your power to change them.

Your thoughts about love? Yours.

Your feelings and emotions around love? Also yours.

Your actions when it comes to love? You guessed it, yours.

So if you're out here waiting for love, chasing love, or wondering why love keeps passing you by, you might want to check what you're expanding. Because love isn't a thing you get. It's a thing you create and radiate from the inside out.

I know, I know. That idea used to tick me off, too. You may even be saying, "Great, just what I need, another guru idea telling me that everything is inside me and that I just need to 'raise my vibration,' find my 'who,' feel the feels, or some other fluffy nonsense." Meanwhile, you're here doing everything *right*.

- App-hopping, playing the love lottery, dating, trying . . .

- Doing the work, going to therapy, and even taking every free online webinar on self help and self awareness that every coach has to offer
- Showing up, being open, following all the damn "rules"

And yet, nothing.

I remember when I heard, "You attract what you believe." I wanted to throw a damn chair.

Because of my belief? *I wanted love.* That's what I believed! How the hell could my thoughts and beliefs be the issue when I was so clear about what I wanted?

Then, one day, I got it.

Not when I was dating. Not during the heartbreaks. Not even when I got married to an incredible man who shows up for me in ways I didn't know were possible. It came later, in the quiet of my learning stage, when I finally had the space to sit with what was still running the show underneath it all. A memory surfaced. A man from my past I once thought I wanted.

He wasn't emotionally unavailable; he was *logistically* unavailable. He was in a relationship. And the woman he was with? She was his status. His financial anchor. His image. Me? I was his emotional companion. The "bonus." The one he called when he needed depth but not commitment. Connection but not clarity. And I let it happen. Because somewhere inside me, I believed that was love. I believed being "chosen" meant waiting. Proving. Being second. Not second to another woman, but second to the *role*. Second to his needs. Second to his life. Because the belief I had been expanding wasn't just about him; it was about what I thought love required of me: That the man comes first. That the wife comes second. That my role was to adapt, to support, to shrink, to not be fully seen. And let's be honest, I didn't invent that belief. It was passed down. Woven into the stories, the systems, and the silences in which I was raised.

I come from a lineage of women who loved hard, worked harder, and still came second.

Second to the man. Second to the family. Second to survival. Because survival came first—not joy, not rest, not dreams. They didn't have the luxury of asking *what do I want?* They were too busy holding it all together. Their love was strong, but it came with sacrifice. And somewhere along the way, I learned that love meant losing pieces of yourself to earn your place.

But I'm not here to repeat that story. I'm here to rewrite it.

That belief didn't disappear just because I got married. It still showed up in moments where I hesitated to speak up, to take up space, to ask for more. Not because I wasn't loved. But because I hadn't yet fully believed I was allowed to receive love *differently*.

That's when it hit me:

Wanting love ≠ Believing in love.

Because wanting it, crying for it, chasing it, dating for it, even marrying into it doesn't mean you believe you're *worthy* of it. Not the watered-down version. The real thing. Love that holds you as a whole, not as an accessory. That was my pattern. And the moment I saw it, I could finally interrupt it. Not to shame who I had been . . . but to finally choose who I was becoming. And that choice? It didn't come without resistance. Because even as I consciously reached for something better, something truer . . . my subconscious still had something to say. My conscious mind was screaming, "Yes, I want love!" But my subconscious—that deep-rooted, behind-the-scenes programming? It was whispering, "You're not lovable. Love always hurts. Relationships are exhausting. If you open up, you'll get hurt." And the big one: "You're a woman, so what you say doesn't really matter in the long run. It's about the head of the household. The man."

And guess what? That sneaky little voice inside me? It was running the whole damn show.

I once believed that finding the right man would complete me. I was sold the fantasy early. That once I found "the one," life would click into place. I'd feel whole. Seen. Safe. So I chased it. I jumped headfirst into relationships that looked promising but always ended the same way. I ignored the gut nudges. Dismissed the red flags. I confused chaos for chemistry, inconsistency for mystery, and intensity for intimacy. I painted potential over people who weren't actually aligned. Not because I was naive, but because I was programmed. My subconscious was trying to resolve old wounds with new people. And it never worked. Not once.

It took me years, literal years, to realize that love isn't about someone choosing you. It's about you choosing yourself first.

Real love isn't about being *completed* by someone. It's about expanding into your fullness. Love begins with what you believe and expands with what you allow. Here's what I wish someone had told me sooner: Our subconscious beliefs, often formed way back in childhood, can shape our adult relationships in profound, often invisible ways.

If you were hurt, ignored, or made to feel small and you didn't receive the comfort, safety, or support you needed? You may have internalized beliefs like:

"If I open up, I'll be rejected."

"Love means sacrifice."

"Relationships are dangerous."

"Being loved means being needed—not being known."

And without realizing it, those beliefs became your compass. Not because they're true, but because they were familiar. But the magic? Once you see them, you can change them. That's the power of self-expansion. Not chasing something outside of you . . . but turning inward to redefine you and rewrite the script.

If expansion is inevitable, then you better believe your beliefs are expanding, too. Not the ones you journal about on New Year's Day. I'm talking about the ones running quietly in the background when no one's watching.

The belief that says, "Love has to be earned."

The belief that says, "If I let go, I'll be abandoned."

The belief that says, "Being chosen is the goal."

Those aren't just thoughts. They're scripts. They're patterns. And they're architects of your reality. But you're not here to keep building a house on foundations you didn't choose. You're here to interrupt that damn story. Because expansion? She's not waiting on you to feel ready. She's already moving. The only question is: Are you expanding the truth of who you are? Or the lie of who you've been told to be?

This isn't just about calling yourself out; it's about calling yourself forward. Forward into the version of you that isn't afraid to name what's no longer serving you. Forward into the kind of love that starts inside, not outside. Forward into the clarity that says, "I decide what expands from here." Now go get honest with your beliefs—because that's where the real expansion begins.

THOUGHT SHIFTER

Your Belief Is Showing

Grab your journal, notes app, sticky notes—whatever works—and take ten uninterrupted minutes to meet your mind where it's really at. Go raw. No sugar coating. This is the gold.

Ask yourself:

1. What do I *really* believe about love?

_____

_____

_____

_____

_____

_____

2. What's a belief about myself I've been unconsciously expanding?

_____

_____

_____

_____

3. Who taught me what love is—and do I still agree with them?

_____

_____

_____

_____

4. What belief am I *done* expanding starting today?

_____

_____

_____

_____

5. What belief am I choosing to expand instead?

_____

_____

_____

_____

Let this be your pattern interrupt. Your permission slip. Your next-level truth. Because when you shift your beliefs, you shift your life.

. . . .

CHAPTER 23

THE INNER SABOTEUR

THAT SNEAKY LITTLE $H!T IN YOUR HEAD

The inner saboteur isn't going away just because you "worked on it once" or read this chapter. It's not a one-and-done healing moment. It's more like an annoying neighbor who keeps knocking, louder—especially when you're tired, vulnerable, or reaching for something bigger than you've ever believed possible. Some people call it their gremlin. Some call it self doubt. I call it what it is, your inner saboteur. That sneaky little $h!t in your head who shows up the moment you start expanding toward what you actually want.

And the closer you get to real expansion? The louder that saboteur gets because it doesn't want you free. It wants you safe. Safe in the smallness. Safe in the familiar. Safe in the same old loop it's been spinning for years. But safety isn't the same as freedom.

That voice in your head might sound like "just being realistic," but it's often just fear in a trench coat pretending to protect you. It's not your truth; it's your trauma in disguise. An old belief system masquerading as your gut instinct.

And your power? It lies in questioning it because even the strongest hearts second guess love. It doesn't matter how smart you are, how respected you are, or how many degrees hang on your wall; your inner saboteur doesn't care. It'll still whisper, "You're too much" or "You'll end up alone.

Dr. Victoria Thompson, emergency room physician, life-saver, badass, and longtime friend, was the walking definition of high-functioning. Calm under pressure, a leader among peers, the kind of woman you'd want by your side in an actual apocalypse. And yet? Even she had a sneaky little $h!t of her own.

When she was offered a career-defining promotion, a statewide leadership role to transform emergency protocols, everyone assumed she'd be over the moon. But she wasn't. She panicked. Not about the job. About love.

"I don't know if I should take it," she told me, coffee clutched in her hand, eyes scanning the table like she was trying to find a safe exit. "What if this creates distance between me and Derek? What if he thinks I'm choosing my ambition over him?"

Derek was her partner at the time, steady, loyal, good on paper. But deep down, Victoria had a history. A pattern. Every time she started to shine, she'd shrink. Not because of the work, but because of the fear that shining too brightly would burn the relationship down. She'd been told before she was "too driven," "intimidating," "emasculating." And those comments stuck like little seeds of shame that bloomed every time she got close to something great.

And there it was, Victoria's inner saboteur in action. Not saying "you're not capable." But saying "you'll be alone if you are."

She'd worked her entire life to be where she was. And now, just as she stood at the edge of expansion, her fear was louder than ever. "I don't want to sabotage this," she whispered, "but I don't want to lose myself either." We sat in that moment. And then, slowly, she started to untangle the story. What if this wasn't about Derek at all? What if the real fear was that she'd outgrow the relationship? That the emotional weight of making herself smaller for him was already starting to feel like a burden? Love that requires you to dim your light isn't love. It's a contract of survival. And Victoria? She was finally done surviving.

Victoria made the pivot, and that changed everything. She took the job. She didn't downplay it, soften it, or apologize for it. She took it with her full chest, knowing it might shift the relationship. And guess what? It did.

Derek wasn't thrilled. He grew distant. Made subtle jabs. Started pulling away. And when the inevitable "what are we doing here?" conversation came, Victoria chose herself. Not because she didn't care. But because for the first time ever, she cared more about not abandoning *herself* than being left by someone else.

While this reads like a romcom, you can't make this shit up! Six months later, on a policy panel in D.C., she met someone new. A fellow doctor. Equally driven. Equally kind. And completely unbothered by her brilliance. In her words, "I didn't know men like this existed."

Victoria never would've met him if she'd stayed small for someone who wasn't meant to go where she was headed. She chose to stay aligned with herself and no one or nothing else.

Victoria's story isn't about climbing a ladder. It's about not shrinking for the sake of connection. She faced her saboteur, "I'm too much for love," and rewrote the script. She expanded in love by expanding into her truth. And she learned this: When you stop trying to make yourself the right size for the wrong people, the right ones show up.

Your inner saboteur thrives in the shadows, when you don't notice it, when you don't question it, when you just accept its whispers as truth. But when you call it out? When you shine a big, bold light on its lies? It loses its power. That's what Victoria did. And now it's your turn.

SABOTEUR REFRAME: FLIP THE SCRIPT AND TAKE YOUR POWER BACK

Next time that sneaky shit shows up, try this:

1. **Pause. Name it:** "Oh, hey, ya little $h!t" (or actually give it a name you identify with) "I see you."
2. **Ask:** Is this voice trying to keep me safe . . . or stuck?

3. **Ask again:** Is this *actually true* or just *historically familiar?*
4. **Reframe it:** "This might be hard, but I'm safe to try."
5. **Act anyway:** Expansion doesn't need permission from your past to move forward.

Now breathe. You just did something most people never do: You named the pattern and met it with power. This is the work. This is how you expand yourself into what you want. Not by "thinking positively." Not by slapping on a mantra. Not by ignoring the feelings and pretending they don't matter. But by *seeing* the patterns. *Catching* the thoughts. And *deciding*, right here, right now, that they don't get to run the show anymore.

Once you spot your saboteur in action, ask yourself whether you're ready to stop letting it make the rules. Sound familiar? Yeah. It's wild. Conditioned thoughts and inherited perceptions control everything *until you decide to see them.* Until you decide to take your power back. Because once you *see* the pattern, you *own* the pattern. And once you *own* it? You can change the damn thing.

UNPACKING THE EMOTIONAL BAGGAGE THAT'S BLOCKING YOUR LOVE

You've seen the way thoughts fuel emotions, emotions drive actions, and actions reinforce beliefs. And those beliefs? They become your worldview. They shape *everything.* But what happens when those beliefs are buried under years of emotional clutter? What happens when you're dragging around pain that was never yours to carry in the first place?

You know what happens. You bring it with you, into conversations, into connections, into your next relationship. You carry it like a suitcase with a busted wheel; it clunks, sticks, slows you down, and no matter how hard you try, you can't glide forward with ease.

We hold onto old wounds, betrayals, fears, guilt, shame, resentment, rejection—the whole damn grab bag of life's hard knocks. We think we need them. We think they keep us safe. But all they really do? Weigh us down.

THE STORY OF THE BAGGAGE WE REFUSE TO LET GO

Imagine this…

You've met someone new. They feel different in the best way. You're hopeful. Hopeful enough to dream. So you plan a trip together. You each pack your bags. At the airport, you roll up to check yours, easy, breezy. No shame in bringing your stuff . . . because hey, we all have stuff.

But your partner? They're clutching their bags like their life depends on it. All carry-ons. No check-ins. White-knuckled grip. You offer to help. They flinch. You reassure them. They double down. They tell you about their aunt who had her bags stolen once. Lost everything. Nothing was ever recovered. She even lost her identity, and it took years to get that restored.

You get it. Kind of. So you move over to make room. You scooch as close to the edge as you can, thinking, *No biggie.* But then . . . the flight takes off. And those bags? They're everywhere. Crammed under your feet, their feet. Taking up space. Blocking legroom. Jamming the overhead bins. You purposely checked your bag so you wouldn't have to carry anything, and suddenly, you're not enjoying the ride. You're managing their stuff.

Dinner's awkward. The hotel feels tense. They won't go anywhere without the bags. They sleep with one eye open. You didn't sign up for this. You signed up for connection, joy, and adventure. And instead? You're babysitting baggage. Sound dramatic? Play this out in real life:

THE EMOTIONAL BAGGAGE WE CARRY IN LOVE

You meet someone. The chemistry hits. Conversation flows. It feels easy . . . at first. But somewhere along the way, the bags appear.

Maybe it's abandonment.

Maybe it's insecurity.

Maybe it's hyper-independence masked as strength.

Maybe it's an entire damn trunk full of trust issues.

And now, instead of building something real, you're working over-time to tiptoe around trauma. You're not falling in love; you're stepping into emotional triage. And this, my friend, is where most relationships go to die. Not because the people are bad, but because the *baggage* is unclaimed. Because no one said, "Hey, maybe I don't need to carry all of this anymore."

What's in your bags? How might you unpack them before the trip?

You're reading this chapter for a reason. Something in you is ready. Ready to see what's there. Ready to ask: *Why am I still carrying this?*

Maybe it's:

- That one relationship that shattered your sense of self
- That parent who made you feel invisible
- That best friend who bailed when you needed them most
- That breakup that taught you love equals loss

It's time to unpack what no longer serves you.

And listen, I know . . . you were taught to hold onto it. Conditioned to believe that if you let go, you'll be unprotected. But what if the very thing you're clinging to is what's keeping you from flying? Are your bags filled with fear, distrust, and unresolved pain?

I hope you have this branded or tattooed on you by now: What you carry is what you expand, and what you expand is what you attract.

When you start releasing, piece by piece, and making room? That's when love flows.

That's when your capacity expands. That's when everything shifts.

BAGGAGE CHECK CHALLENGE: WHAT'S IN YOUR BAGS?

1. Name the top three emotional wounds you're still holding onto.
2. *Be real. Be bold. No judgment here.*
3. For each wound, ask: What belief is attached to this?
4. *(Example: "I was cheated on.", "No one is trustworthy.")*
5. Look at your life: How does this belief appear in your relationships?
6. *Get honest. That's where the power is.*
7. Now ask: What would it feel like to leave just *one* of those bags behind?

Write it out. Imagine the lightness. Imagine the freedom.

The best way to change a behavior is to observe it. The best way to shift a habit is to track the habit. It's not about forcing change. It's about noticing. Most of us don't even realize what we're doing until the habit is already in full swing, autopilot activated. That's your subconscious. It's not evil. It's efficient. But it'll run the same loop until you stop it.

That bag of chips when you're sad?

That text you send when you're lonely?

That avoidance when you're scared?

They're not flaws. They're patterns.

And the minute you pause and ask "why do I do this?"

Your awareness superpower has just been engaged for a power-FULL shift.

That's the moment your inner saboteur gets quiet. That's the moment your baggage loses weight. That's the moment your life starts expanding from a place of truth.

THOUGHT SHIFTER

Saboteur Slayer + Baggage Drop

Journal on this:

1. What's one thought I believed today that wasn't actually true?
2. Where did my saboteur show up? What lie did it whisper?
3. What emotion is still living in me from a past wound that hasn't been unpacked?
4. What am I afraid will happen if I actually let it go?
5. What's one thing I'm ready to release—even if it's just one small carry-on—so love has more room to move?

You don't need to unpack everything at once. You just need to unzip the first bag. That's how expansion begins. One thought. One choice. One moment of truth at a time.

. . . .

CHAPTER 24

BREAKING THE CYCLE

OBSERVING, INTERRUPTING,
AND REWIRING HABITS

The best way to change a behavior? Observe it.

The best way to change a habit? Track it.

Simple? Yes. Easy? Hell no. And heck, most of us don't even *notice* our habits until they've got us by the throat, running our lives like a sneaky little control freak in the background. That's not a personality flaw. That's your subconscious doing exactly what it's wired to do: automate, conserve energy, and protect you.

Here's where it can get tricky: Your subconscious doesn't care if the habit is helping you or hurting you. It just runs the program it was given.

Tie your shoes? Habit. Brush your teeth? Habit. Stress snack a whole bag of chips? Scroll your ex's socials like a crime scene? Or pick a fight because you're scared of getting too close? Also habits.

It's not you failing. It's your subconscious defaulting.

But here's the turning point, the moment you wake up and go, "Wait . . . why the hell do I do this every time that happens?"

And that's it. That's the reclaiming moment. The second you observe the pattern is the second you regain your power. And now? You get to update the programming.

You can't change what you can't see, and that's why observation is the first power move you can make. The subconscious is slick. It loves to stay behind the curtain, pulling levers while you think you're in control. But once you observe it? The lights come on. The trigger is revealed. And once you see the trigger? You can interrupt it.

MIKE AND HIS COMMUTE RAGE

It turns out that years ago, Mike had a boss who treated being one minute late like a felony. There were passive-aggressive emails, meetings that started without him, and cold stares that said, "You're replaceable."

It wasn't feedback; it was a slow bleed of psychological warfare.

So Mike's brain adapted. Late didn't mean delayed; it meant unsafe. Traffic didn't mean congestion; it meant failure. The commute? It became a trigger zone.

Fast-forward to now. Mike runs his *own* business. Nobody's clocking him. Nobody's waiting to reprimand him. And yet, every morning in traffic, his nervous system still lights up like it's twenty years ago and his job's on the line. That rage? It wasn't about the cars. It was about the shame.

Unspoken. Unprocessed. Still unhealed. And that's what's so wild: Your subconscious doesn't check timestamps. It doesn't ask, "Is this still true?" It runs the old script: protects, defends, explodes, and calls it personality. But that's not who Mike *is*. That's just the part of him that never got updated. And this is the part often left out: If you don't rewrite the story, your past will keep dragging you by the throat into your present.

So what about you? You've seen how it plays out. Now it's time to turn the mirror back on you. Ready to break your own pattern? Here's the reboot that puts you back in the driver's seat:

THE THREE-STEP PATTERN REBOOT

Here's how to break the cycle. *Real-life brain rewiring*, not wishful thinking.

Step 1: Observe the Habit

Become the curious detective of your own behavior.
 Ask:

- When does this pattern show up?
- What triggers it? Stress? Fear? A person? A vibe?
- What emotion hits right before, during, or after?
- What's the payoff? (Yes, even sabotaging habits bring comfort or control.)

Awareness is your power move. Name it to tame it.

Step 2: Interrupt the Cycle

You don't need to change everything—just enough to disrupt the autopilot.

- Stress eating? Pause and walk the driveway first.
- Getting defensive when criticized? Breathe. Respond with curiosity.
- Procrastinating? Set a timer for five minutes. Start ugly.

Tiny interruptions are huge rewiring moments. You're breaking the "same old, same old" and forcing your brain to *re-decide*.

Step 3: Rewire the Pattern

Here's where you drop the old loop and choose a new one.
 Ask:

- What do I want to feel instead?

- What behavior or thought aligns with that?
- How do I practice it until it becomes the new automatic?

Your brain doesn't prioritize your joy; it prioritizes what's familiar. But you? You're about to make "healthy, connected, aligned" the new familiar. And that, my friend, is how you expand in love, not protection.

Your subconscious will fight it at first. It'll whisper, "Too hard. Too weird. Let's just do it the old way."

But you're stronger than that voice. You're the one steering now.

THOUGHT SHIFTER

Pattern Pause + Rewire Practice

This exercise is designed to help you *track, challenge, and choose* your next move with intention instead of habit.

1. Track It:

For three days, jot down **one** behavior or reaction you want to shift (avoidance, control, defensiveness, etc.).

Each time it shows up, write:

- What triggered it?
- What emotion came up?
- What did you *do*?
- What was the payoff (comfort, protection, attention, etc.)?

_____

_____

_____

_____

_____

2. Pattern Pause:

Choose one of those moments and reflect:

- What belief is sitting underneath this habit? (Examples: "If I don't fix this, I'll be rejected"; "If I speak up, I'll be attacked"; "If I slow down, I'll fall behind.")
- Is this belief actually true or just *old and familiar*?

_____

_____

_____

_____

_____

3. Rewire It:

Now create a new micro-choice:

- What could I try *instead*?
- What emotion do I want to feel instead?
- What's one tiny action I could repeat until it becomes my new default?

_____

_____

_____

_____

_____

The pattern I'm ready to break is . . .

_____

_____

_____

_____

_____

The belief keeping it alive is . . .

_____

_____

_____

_____

_____

The truth I'm choosing instead is . . .

_____

_____

_____

_____

_____

You're not your old story. You're the one who rewrites it.

CHAPTER 25

LOVE IS AN INSIDE JOB

By now, you've done some serious digging. You've exposed sub-conscious beliefs, faced down your little $h!t inner saboteur, unpacked emotional baggage, and interrupted habits that were running your love life on autopilot. You've started to observe, question, and rewire what you thought love was and how you thought it was supposed to show up.

This isn't surface-level self-help. This is expansion work. And if you're still here, you've already done more than most people ever will. You now know what most don't: Love isn't something you chase. It's something you *are*. But I get it, you might still be asking, "Okay . . . but how do I actually *be* love?" Let's talk about it, but not in theory, in practice.

Imagine your love life—romantic, platonic, self-love, all of it—as a movie. And up until now? Your subconscious has been ghostwriting the script. But what happens when you finally take back the pen?

Meet Ethan and walk with him through the rewrite.

STEP ONE: GET HONEST ABOUT THE LOVE YOU'RE EXPANDING

Ethan didn't think he had love "issues." Divorced for five years. Co-parenting respectfully. Had a stable job, good friendships, and a schedule that kept him moving. He figured that was enough. Until one night, scrolling on his phone in a quiet house, he realized something: *He was expanding loneliness.* Not on purpose, but in the way he avoided deeper conversations. In how he'd convince himself he didn't need intimacy anymore. In how he said yes to women who needed him but never really saw him. His life looked connected, but his energy told the truth: He was protecting, not participating.

THOUGHT SHIFTER

If I fully believed I was already loved and worthy, how would I show up differently in my relationships today?

STEP TWO: ACT FROM LOVE, NOT FOR IT

The following weekend, Ethan found himself texting someone he used to date. She was kind but emotionally chaotic, always needing saving, always praising him for being "so solid." It made him feel important . . . for a moment. As his thumb hovered over the send button, something new surfaced: *Am I texting her because I want to connect? Or because I want to feel needed?*

He set the phone down. He made himself dinner, sat outside, and let the quiet feel like company instead of absence. In that moment, he stopped trying to perform to earn love; he became it.

THOUGHT SHIFTER

Am I doing this because I truly want to or because I'm looking for approval, safety, or a pat on the head?

STEP THREE: CREATE LOVE IN THE TINY, ORDINARY MOMENTS

That week, Ethan tried something radical: *He slowed down.* He gave himself five minutes in the morning to stand still with his coffee. He looked at himself in the mirror and said, "You're allowed to want more." He didn't rush to fix anyone else's problem at work. He didn't explain away his needs. Love wasn't a grand gesture. It was a hundred small moments where he chose presence over performance. And for the first time in years, he felt peace instead of pressure in his chest.

THOUGHT SHIFTER

Where can I create love today for no other reason than that it's who I am?

STEP FOUR: STOP WAITING. START WRITING YOUR LOVE STORY NOW.

That Friday night, Ethan took a notebook and wrote a different kind of story. It wasn't about who he used to be. It wasn't about what he regretted. It was a vision. A love story with wholeness at the center, not rescue, not roles. A story where he no longer had to earn love through emotional labor or fix what was never his to carry. And even though he wasn't dating anyone . . . even though nothing looked different on the outside . . . he felt different. Because for the first time, he believed:

> *Love doesn't start when someone else chooses me. It starts when I stop leaving myself behind.*

THOUGHT SHIFTER

If love were a feeling I carried every day, what would my life look like?

The Love Expansion Challenge

Your mission (if you choose to accept it):

1. Pick One Way to Be Love Today

Maybe it's saying no, holding space, or looking yourself in the mirror without flinching.

_____

_____

_____

_____

_____

2. Document the Shift

At the end of the day, journal: How did I feel? What changed in how I showed up, gave, or received love?

_____

_____

_____

_____

_____

3. Repeat. Expand. Become.

_____

_____

_____

_____

_____

_____

This isn't a one-time task. It's a new identity. Love is a practice, not a destination.

Welcome to the future of love work, not just a mindset, but full-body integration. And you are ready. You are the love you've been waiting for. Forget the motivational fluff. This is an energetic truth. You can't receive more love out there than you're willing to live in here. So stop waiting. Don't just crave it. Be it. Don't just seek it. Radiate it. Don't just wish for it.

Choose it. Every day.

Now go write your love story. Your way. With your whole heart. On your mark, get set . . . expand.

READY TO KEEP GOING?

The portal's waiting with guided breath work, integration practices, and space to bring this work fully into your body.

You've expanded the page. Now expand your practice.

THE
INTEGRATING
FACTOR

· · · · · · · · ·

EXPANDING
WHAT YOU CAME
HERE FOR

As you grab your chair, breathe, and claim your next level, there's one question you need to ask, one that could change everything if you let it: **What if this is as good as it gets?**

It's a question that can either paralyze you or set you free. Most people hear it and feel panic tighten in their chest. Like, *Wait, what?! This can't be it. I'm not done yet. I haven't even started yet!* And that's because you were never meant to settle into your current reality. You were meant to expand through it.

But here's the catch most people miss: *If you can't find peace right where you are, you won't magically find it "over there" either.*

Expansion isn't about hating where you are. It's about loving yourself enough to outgrow it. It's about being able to say, "I honor this season for what it taught me. And I honor myself enough to keep going." Because this moment—even the messy, imperfect, not-what-you-had-planned moment you're standing in—is the foundation for your next.

It's the raw material for your next expansion.

If you can find a little peace here, a little gratitude, a little "I'm still standing, dammit," then you are powerful enough to create something bigger.

You don't expand intentionally by rejecting where you are. You expand by **owning** where you are . . . and choosing where you go next.

The expansion you desire, the one you've been calling for, doesn't shame the starting point. It builds on it. So here's the real question: not "What if this is as good as it gets?" but "What gets to expand because I dared to start from here?" And that's where the real shift happens. Your emotions are your messenger. They tell you exactly where you're aligned and where you're not.

Your energy is your invitation. It's the signal you send before you ever say a word. And your alignment? That's your resume. People feel it. Opportunities respond to it. Life reflects it. You want more success? Practice the energy of success before it shows up. You want deeper love? Live like you're already worthy of it. You want opportunity? Align with possibility, even when your circumstances look the same. You can be standing right next to everything you want and still miss it if your energy isn't tuned to receive it.

What you believe expands.

What you practice becomes your pattern.

What you focus on? That's what finds you.

This isn't about bypassing hard feelings or faking joy.

It's not about settling.

It's about tuning. Aligning. Expanding into the version of you that's ready to receive.

You decide: Does it stay stuck . . . or does it start now?

Breathe that in. Let it land.

Because what if the door isn't locked?

What if it's just waiting for you to move the damn chair?

MOVE THE DAMN CHAIR: THIS IS NOT THE END. THIS IS THE SHIFT.

You made it. Not to the end, but to the beginning of something bigger. Remember back in the Prologue when I said those four little words *move the damn chair* would shift everything?

Well . . . it's time. Buckle up. Breathe it in. This is the moment you realize *you were never stuck.*

You just needed a new seat, a new view, and the courage to move.

By now, you've done more than most people will ever dare. You've dug deep. You've unpacked the subconscious beliefs running your life. You've faced your gremlins, challenged your programming, cracked open your patterns, and chosen to lead from a new place, from the inside out.

You didn't just read a book. You moved through your **life** with honesty. You redefined **leadership** with integrity. And you reclaimed **love** with presence. And now you're standing in the in-between. That sacred moment after awareness and before action.

This is not the end. This is the launch. This is a movement—your movement

THE FIRE, THE SMOKE, AND THE SHIFT

Let me tell you a story. It was one of those unforgettable weekends, a soul-fueled, laughter-soaked, unplug-and-just-be kind of getaway. Riverfront house. Ancient land. Crackling fire pit. Sacred vibes.

The fire, though? Had beef with me. No matter where I sat, the smoke came for me. Eyes burning, lungs gasping, I moved left. I moved right. Still smoke. I flapped. I coughed. I complained. Until finally I stood up, picked up my chair, and walked to the opposite side of the fire pit.

And there it was.

A breathtaking, soul-stilling mountain. A view I never would've seen if I hadn't finally moved my damn chair. I turned to my girl-friends and said, "Y'all . . . look at this. All I had to do was move the damn chair."

And the silence that followed? Sacred. Soul-slap sacred. We all felt it. Because that fire wasn't the problem; it was my refusal to shift my position that kept me in the smoke.

How often do we sit in smoke—in stuck jobs that suck the life out of us, draining relationships, outdated stories—and wait for something outside of us to shift?

But expansion doesn't wait. It moves. It changes your seat, your scene, your center. And this book? It was your practice round. Now it's time to apply the lesson in real life, in real leadership, in real love.

WHAT COULD CHANGE IF YOU MOVED THE DAMN CHAIR?

This is your moment. No fanfare. No drumroll. Where in your **life** have you stayed too long in discomfort hoping it would pass? Where in your **leadership** have you settled for smoke instead of clarity? Where in your **relationships** have you forgotten that movement is your power?

The fire isn't out to get you. It's just showing you where you no longer belong. And the mountain? The truth? The next level you? They've been waiting.

You've already begun the shift. Now it's your turn. Choose how you want to keep moving forward.

1. Write a love letter to yourself.

Let your future self, the fully expanded, deeply aligned version of you, speak to you now.

> Prompt: "Here's what I want you to remember every time you forget who you are . . ."

2. Declare your "I Am" manifesto.

You're not the old patterns. Write your declaration.
Start with:

- I release . . .
- I choose . . .
- I no longer . . .
- I now become . . .

3. Take the thirty-day embodiment challenge.

Pick one micro-action each day that helps you expand in life, leadership, or love. Track it. Reflect on it. Watch what changes.

4. Reflect and reclaim.

Ask yourself:

- What belief did I leave behind?
- What did I step into?
- Who am I now?

_____

_____

_____

_____

_____

_____

_____

_____

_____

_____

_____

_____

_____

_____

5. Move the damn chair.

Literally. Figuratively. Emotionally.

Ask:

- Where am I still sitting in smoke?
- What mountain have I not looked up to see?
- What would a shift—even a small one—do for my peace, power, and purpose?

This isn't one-and-done work. This is forever work. Eternal work. And because expansion is a lifelong practice, I've built a space to support you beyond these pages. Go to www.TheExpansionFactor.com and bookmark it. You'll find video guides, tools, practices, and integration tracks to keep expanding. The tools are there when you need them. The practices are waiting when you're ready. But remember, transformation doesn't happen from collecting information. It happens when you choose to move, when you choose to engage, when you choose to expand.

Which brings us here . . . don't just *read* the work. **Live** it.

You are not stuck.

You are not broken.

You are not behind.

You are seated in smoke. And your only job now . . . is to rise, shift, and look up.

Because peace is waiting.

Perspective is waiting.

You don't have to have it all figured out. You just have to move.

So on your mark . . .

Grab your chair.

Take a breath.

And move it. **Move the damn chair.**

This isn't the end—it's the beginning. Scan here to enter my private portal, where I've gathered my best tools to support your journey forward—my gift to you, with gratitude.

ACKNOWLEDGEMENTS

"WHAT GOT YOU HERE WON'T GET YOU THERE."
—MARSHALL GOLDSMITH

Ain't that the truth.

This book would not exist without two pivotal conversations.

The first happened in the training room at City BBQ when Mike Muldoon, CEO, looked at me and asked, "Deb, when is your book coming out?" I laughed and said, "It's in the works." And it was… just not this one. But his question planted the seed that kept pushing at me until I couldn't ignore it anymore.

The second came about a year later, Jenelle Kruse and Arelis Romero, you saw me. You knew me. And you didn't hesitate to challenge me to level up when I thought I was already playing full out. You reminded me of what I ask from others and called me to demand it of myself. This road hasn't been smooth. But it's been a consistent, soul-level teacher in the art of redefining and letting go of what no longer serves. I'm deeply thankful to both of you for showing up with your courage.

To my amazing kiddos, Josh, Rachel, Jonathan, and Salem, you have been and will always be my greatest teachers. I didn't get a manual for parenting (and let's be honest, I probably wouldn't have read it anyway). I did the best I could, and still . . . I fell short; I stumbled; and some may even say, "I got it wrong". But through it all, your love, grace, and presence remain unwavering. I am honored and proud to be your mom.

To my Jason,

You're my "s," and I'm your "u" in *us*. . Cheesy? Maybe for some, but it's *us*, and I only want to *"live it us-ly"* with you.

The hours you've spent reading, editing, cooking, refilling water bottles, delivering meals to my desk—all while running our farm and a full-time job of your own—I see it all. **You are the expanded magic in my life.** You've held the space for me to shed every layer that no longer serves me without ever trying to fix or change me. Our conversations, our tears, our belly laughs, our flare-ups—every single one has shaped this journey. You've learned my red-green, catabolic-anabolic language, and you use it with me and for me. You're my example. And I'm so wildly, forever grateful that you found me.

To Tricia, from your Jira, I love you forever and beyond. *I'm giddy too*, with excitement for all that's now and next. You're my eternal.

To every soul who has walked this path with me, whether for a moment or a lifetime, you've played your role exquisitely well. **Don't stop. Don't shrink. Your best is enough, and I'm honored to witness your becoming.**

And to my six beautiful grands, Gammie loves you deeply. You are the legacy, the light, and the reminder that this life, this love, this expansion, is always worth it.

ABOUT THE AUTHOR

For most of my life, I believed expansion meant growth toward the good—the things we want, dream of, and strive for. More purpose. More success. More love. That belief held strong . . . until it shattered. What cracked me open wasn't failure. It was revelation. A soul truth so undeniable, so piercing that it stripped away every shallow definition I'd clung to. And in its place? A new understanding that didn't ask politely. It demanded change, not later, not someday, but *now*.

What I realized is this: You're always expanding something. And until you become conscious of what you're expanding, you'll keep reinforcing the very patterns you're trying to break.

It happened during a leadership training I was facilitating at our Expansion Leadership Academy. I was deep in the flow, teaching one of our core, no-compromise truths, a principle that lives at the heart of everything we do at Cultural Alignment Solutions: **"You are always leading. What are you leading?"** Those eight words shape every conversation we have with leaders because if you don't know what you're leading with—your energy, your beliefs, your reactions—then chances are fear is leading. Discontent is leading. Self-doubt is running the show. And everything around you is following its cue.

And then it happened. In a moment that felt like lightning splitting through the ordinary, a phrase dropped out of my mouth, clear, raw, and louder than I intended, but it didn't come from my mind. It came from something deeper. Something ancient and electric in my soul: **"You are always expanding. What are you expanding?"**

The room went still. No fidgeting. No note taking. Just breath and silence. Because it hit.

Not just for them. For me. That sentence cracked something wide open, a knowing so strong, I couldn't unhear it. Couldn't unfeel it. It wasn't planned. It wasn't polished. But it was *truth*, the kind that rearranges everything.

That one sentence became a portal. Not just a mic-drop moment, but a new lens. A new way of seeing. A new way of *being*. That moment is what birthed this book.

Expansion is a verb. A force. A frequency. It's not good or bad. It just is. You're expanding right now, in this breath, belief, and choice. We expand whatever we feed. Whatever we repeat. Whatever we give our energy to, consciously or not. So if you're constantly choosing from fear? You're expanding fear. If you're acting from the belief that you're not worthy, not chosen, not enough? That belief gets bigger. Louder. Heavier. And your life starts to reflect it. That's the part no one tells you. You're not stuck. You're just unconsciously expanding what no longer serves you. That's where it hit me; I had to ask a different question. I started asking myself, "If I make this choice . . . what am I expanding?"

I now give this same question to my clients to ask themselves. If you can feel peace in your body, ease in your energy, and truth in your breath, then *know* this: You're expanding alignment. You're expanding your next level, and you're expanding on purpose. Expansion isn't a trend. It's not some fluffy self-help slogan.

It's a mirror and a megaphone for your energy. And once you learn how to work with it consciously? Everything changes.

A few months after that soul-splitting moment, my team turned the mirror back on me. "Debbie," they asked, "what are *you* doing to expand at the level you ask of your clients?"

I laughed, shrugged, and said what most high-functioning achievers say: "We're good. Life's already great." But they didn't let me off the hook. They pushed. They held me to my standard.

And thank God they did. Because if I hadn't taken that challenge seriously, I know this book wouldn't exist. I would've expanded comfort instead of courage. Settled for good . . . while greatness stood at the door, knocking.

This book is the result of that choice. It's not theory. It's not fluff. It's the lived, breathed, bruised, and breakthrough version of me poured onto these pages. Every word has been lived.

Every lesson earned. Every sentence comes from the front lines of expansion. I've been the one who felt unseen, shushed, emotionally exhausted, mentally burned out, and disconnected from my own worth. I've had to *remember* who I am. *Rewire* what I believed. *Redefine* what life, leadership, and love look like when you show up rooted in truth, full of energy and stripped of performance.

I've stood at the mystic door, one hand on what's familiar, the other on what's possible. And I chose to open it. So here we are. This book isn't just a read; it's the opportunity for a return, a reclamation, a revolution. This is your door, your mirror for your movement.

Welcome to your expansion, not just toward what you want . . . but into the fullness of who you truly are.

www.ingramcontent.com/pod-product-compliance
Lightning Source LLC
Chambersburg PA
CBHW021229130626
46554CB00004B/1409